ALSO BY JACQUELINE WOODSON

Last Summer with Maizon

The Dear One

Maizon at Blue Hill

Between Madison and Palmetto

I Hadn't Meant to Tell You This

From the Notebooks of Melanin Sun

The House You Pass on the Way

If You Come Softly

Lena

Miracle's Boys

Hush

Locomotion

Behind You

Feathers

After Tupac and D Foster

Peace, Locomotion

Beneath a Meth Moon

brown girl dreaming

JACQUELINE WOODSON

Nancy Paulsen Books ◉ An Imprint of Penguin Group (USA)

NANCY PAULSEN BOOKS
Published by the Penguin Group
Penguin Group (USA) LLC
375 Hudson Street, New York, NY 10014

(Ω)

USA | Canada | UK | Ireland | Australia
New Zealand | India | South Africa | China
penguin.com
A Penguin Random House Company

Library of Congress Cataloging-in-Publication Data is available upon request.

Printed in the United States of America.
ISBN 978-0-399-25251-8
10 9 8 7

Design by Ryan Thomann. Text set in Garth Graphic.

This book is for my family—
past, present and future.
With love.

 CONTENTS

WOODSON FAMILY TREE

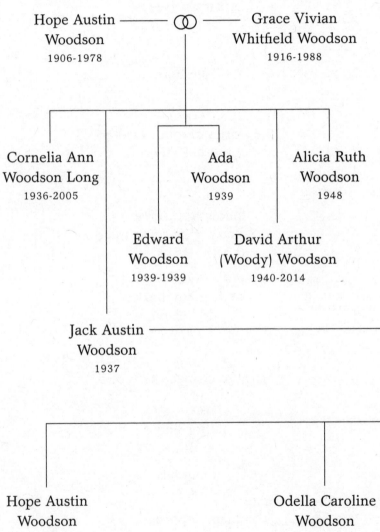

Hope Austin
Woodson
1906-1978

⊙

Grace Vivian
Whitfield Woodson
1916-1988

Cornelia Ann
Woodson Long
1936-2005

Ada
Woodson
1939

Alicia Ruth
Woodson
1948

Edward
Woodson
1939-1939

David Arthur
(Woody) Woodson
1940-2014

Jack Austin
Woodson
1937

Hope Austin
Woodson
1960

Odella Caroline
Woodson
1961

IRBY FAMILY TREE

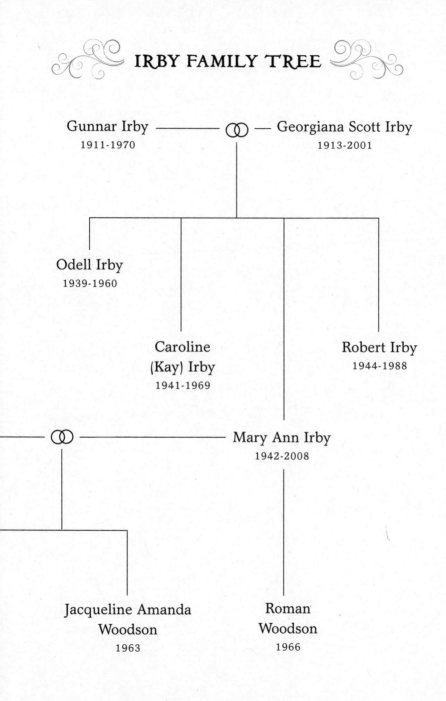

Gunnar Irby
1911-1970

Georgiana Scott Irby
1913-2001

Odell Irby
1939-1960

Caroline
(Kay) Irby
1941-1969

Robert Irby
1944-1988

Mary Ann Irby
1942-2008

Jacqueline Amanda
Woodson
1963

Roman
Woodson
1966

Hold fast to dreams
For if dreams die
Life is a broken-winged bird
That cannot fly.

Hold fast to dreams
For when dreams go
Life is a barren field
Frozen with snow.

—Langston Hughes

PART I

i am born

february 12, 1963

I am born on a Tuesday at University Hospital
Columbus, Ohio,
USA—
a country caught

between Black and White.

I am born not long from the time
or far from the place
where
my great-great-grandparents
worked the deep rich land
unfree
dawn till dusk
unpaid
drank cool water from scooped-out gourds
looked up and followed
the sky's mirrored constellation
to freedom.

I am born as the South explodes,
too many people too many years

enslaved, then emancipated
but not free, the people
who look like me
keep fighting
and marching
and getting killed
so that today—
February 12, 1963
and every day from this moment on,
brown children like me can grow up
free. Can grow up
learning and voting and walking and riding
wherever *we* want.

I am born in Ohio but
the stories of South Carolina already run
like rivers
through my veins.

second daughter's
second day on earth

My birth certificate says: Female Negro
Mother: Mary Anne Irby, 22, Negro
Father: Jack Austin Woodson, 25, Negro

In Birmingham, Alabama, Martin Luther King Jr.
    is planning a march on Washington, where
John F. Kennedy is president.
In Harlem, Malcolm X is standing on a soapbox
    talking about a revolution.

Outside the window of University Hospital,
snow is slowly falling. So much already
covers this vast Ohio ground.

In Montgomery, only seven years have passed
    since Rosa Parks refused
to give up
her seat on a city bus.

I am born brown-skinned, black-haired
and wide-eyed.
I am born Negro here and Colored there

and somewhere else,
the Freedom Singers have linked arms,
their protests rising into song:
*Deep in my heart, I do believe
that we shall overcome someday.*

and somewhere else, James Baldwin
is writing about injustice, each novel,
each essay, changing the world.

> *I do not yet know who I'll be
> what I'll say
> how I'll say it . . .*

Not even three years have passed since a brown girl
named Ruby Bridges
walked into an all-white school.
Armed guards surrounded her while hundreds
of white people spat and called her names.

She was six years old.

> *I do not know if I'll be strong like Ruby.
> I do not know what the world will look like
> when I am finally able to walk, speak, write . . .*
> Another Buckeye!
> *the nurse says to my mother.
> Already, I am being named for this place.*

Ohio. The Buckeye State.
My fingers curl into fists, automatically
This is the way, *my mother said,*
of every baby's hand.
I do not know if these hands will become
Malcolm's—raised and fisted
or Martin's—open and asking
or James's—curled around a pen.
I do not know if these hands will be
Rosa's
or Ruby's
gently gloved
and fiercely folded
calmly in a lap,
on a desk,
around a book,
ready
to change the world . . .

a girl named jack

Good enough name for me, my father said
the day I was born.
Don't see why
she can't have it, too.

But the women said no.
My mother first.
Then each aunt, pulling my pink blanket back
patting the crop of thick curls
tugging at my new toes
touching my cheeks.

We won't have a girl named Jack, my mother said.

And my father's sisters whispered,
A boy named Jack was bad enough.
But only so my mother could hear.
Name a girl Jack, my father said,
and she can't help but
grow up strong.
Raise her right, my father said,
and she'll make that name her own.

Name a girl Jack
and people will look at her twice, my father said.

For no good reason but to ask if her parents
were crazy, my mother said.

And back and forth it went until I was Jackie
and my father left the hospital mad.

My mother said to my aunts,
Hand me that pen, wrote
Jacqueline where it asked for a name.
Jacqueline, just in case
someone thought to drop the *ie.*

Jacqueline, just in case
I grew up and wanted something a little bit longer
and further away from
Jack.

the woodsons of ohio

My father's family
can trace their history back
to Thomas Woodson of Chillicothe, said to be
the first son
of Thomas Jefferson and Sally Hemings
some say
this isn't so but . . .

the Woodsons of Ohio know
what the Woodsons coming before them
left behind, in Bibles, in stories,
in history coming down through time

so

ask any Woodson why
you can't go down the Woodson line
without
finding
doctors and lawyers and teachers
athletes and scholars and people in government
they'll say,

We had a head start.
They'll say,
Thomas Woodson expected the best of us.
They'll lean back, lace their fingers
across their chests,
smile a smile that's older than time, say,

Well it all started back before Thomas Jefferson
Woodson of Chillicothe . . .

and they'll begin to tell our long, long story.

the ghosts of the
nelsonville house

The Woodsons are one
of the few Black families in this town, their house
is big and white and sits
on a hill.

Look up
to see them
through the high windows
inside a kitchen filled with the light
of a watery Nelsonville sun. In the parlor
a fireplace burns warmth
into the long Ohio winter.

Keep looking and it's spring again,
the light's gold now, and dancing
across the pine floors.

Once, there were so many children here
running through this house
up and down the stairs, hiding under beds
and in trunks,

sneaking into the kitchen for tiny pieces
of icebox cake, cold fried chicken,
thick slices of their mother's honey ham . . .

Once, my father was a baby here
and then he was a boy . . .

But that was a long time ago.

In the photos my grandfather is taller than everybody
and my grandmother just an inch smaller.

On the walls their children run through fields,
    play in pools,
dance in teen-filled rooms, all of them

grown up and gone now—
but wait!

Look closely:

There's Aunt Alicia, the baby girl,
curls spiraling over her shoulders, her hands
cupped around a bouquet of flowers. Only
four years old in that picture, and already,
a reader.

Beside Alicia another picture, my father, Jack,

the oldest boy.
Eight years old and mad about something
or is it someone
we cannot see?

In another picture, my uncle Woody,
baby boy
laughing and pointing
the Nelsonville house behind him and maybe
his brother at the end of his pointed finger.

My aunt Anne in her nurse's uniform,
my aunt Ada in her university sweater
Buckeye to the bone . . .

The children of Hope and Grace.

Look closely. There I am
in the furrow of Jack's brow,
in the slyness of Alicia's smile,
in the bend of Grace's hand . . .

There I am . . .

Beginning.

it'll be scary sometimes

My great-great-grandfather on my father's side
was born free in Ohio,

1832.

Built his home and farmed his land,
then dug for coal when the farming
wasn't enough. Fought hard
in the war. His name in stone now
on the Civil War Memorial:

William J. Woodson
United States Colored Troops,
Union, Company B 5th Regt.

A long time dead but living still
among the other soldiers
on that monument in Washington, D.C.

His son was sent to Nelsonville
lived with an aunt

William Woodson
the only brown boy in an all-white school.

You'll face this in your life someday,
my mother will tell us
over and over again.
A moment when you walk into a room and

no one there is like you.

It'll be scary sometimes. But think of William Woodson
and you'll be all right.

football dreams

No one was faster
than my father on the football field.
No one could keep him
from crossing the line. Then
touching down again.
Coaches were watching the way he moved,
his easy stride, his long arms reaching
up, snatching the ball from its soft pocket
of air.

My father dreamed football dreams,
and woke to a scholarship
at Ohio State University.
Grown now
living the big-city life
in Columbus
just sixty miles
from Nelsonville
and from there
Interstate 70 could get you
on your way west to Chicago
Interstate 77 could take you south

but my father said
no colored Buckeye in his right mind
would ever want to go there.

From Columbus, my father said,
*you could go just about
anywhere.*

other people's memory

You were born in the morning, Grandma Georgiana said.
I remember the sound of the birds. Mean
old blue jays squawking. They like to fight, you know.
Don't mess with blue jays!
I hear they can kill a cat if they get mad enough.

And then the phone was ringing.
Through all that static and squawking, I heard
your mama telling me you'd come.
Another girl, I stood there thinking,
so close to the first one.
Just like your mama and Caroline. Not even
a year between them and so close, you could hardly tell
where one ended and the other started.
And that's how I know you came in the morning.
That's how I remember.

You came in the late afternoon, my mother said.
Two days after I turned twenty-two.
Your father was at work.
Took a rush hour bus
trying

to get to you. But
by the time he arrived,
you were already here.
He missed the moment, my mother said,
but what else is new.

You're the one that was born near night,
     my father says.
When I saw you, I said, She's the unlucky one
come out looking just like her daddy.
He laughs. *Right off the bat, I told your mama,*
We're gonna call this one after me.

My time of birth wasn't listed
on the certificate, then got lost again
amid other people's bad memory.

no returns

When my mother comes home
from the hospital with me,
my older brother takes one look
inside the pink blanket, says,
Take her back. We already have one of those.

Already three years old and still doesn't understand
how something so tiny and new
can't be returned.

how to listen #1

Somewhere in my brain
each laugh, tear and lullaby
becomes *memory*.

uncle odell

Six months before my big sister is born,
my uncle Odell is hit by a car
while home in South Carolina
on leave from the Navy.

When the phone rang in the Nelsonville house,
maybe my mother was out hanging laundry
on the line or down in the kitchen
speaking softly with her mother-in-law, Grace, missing
her own mama back home.
Maybe the car was packed and ready for the drive
back to Columbus—the place my father
called the Big City—now *their* home.
But every Saturday morning, they drove
the hour to Nelsonville and stayed
till Sunday night.

Maybe right before the phone rang, tomorrow

was just another day.

But when the news of my uncle's dying

traveled from the place he fell in South Carolina,
to the cold March morning in Ohio,
my mother looked out into a gray day
that would change her forever.

Your brother

my mother heard her own mother say
and then there was only a roaring in the air around her
a new pain where once there wasn't pain
a hollowness where only minutes before
she had been whole.

good news

Months before the bone-cold
Buckeye winter settles over Ohio,
the last September light brings

my older sister,

named
Odella Caroline after my uncle Odell
and my aunt Caroline.

In South Carolina, the phone rings.

As my mother's mother moves toward it,
she closes her eyes,
then opens them to look out over her yard.
As she reaches for it,
she watches the way the light slips through
the heavy pine needles, dapples everything
with sweet September light . . .

Her hand on the phone now, she lifts it
praying silently

for the good news
the sweet chill of autumn
is finally bringing her way.

my mother and grace

It is the South that brings my mother
and my father's mother, Grace,
together.
Grace's family is from Greenville, too.
So my mother
is home to her, in a way her own kids
can't understand.
You know how those Woodsons are, Grace says.
The Woodsons this and the North that
making Mama smile, remember
that Grace, too, was someone else before. Remember
that Grace, like my mother, wasn't always a Woodson.

They are *home* to each other, Grace
to my mother is as familiar
as the Greenville air.

Both know that southern way of talking
without words, remember when
the heat of summer
could melt the mouth,
so southerners stayed quiet

looked out over the land,
nodded at what seemed like nothing
but that silent nod said everything
anyone needed to hear.

Here in Ohio, my mother and Grace
aren't afraid
of too much air between words, are happy
just for another familiar body in the room.

But the few words in my mother's mouth
become the *missing*
after Odell dies—a different silence
than either of them has ever known.

I'm sorry about your brother, Grace says.
Guess God needed him back and sent you a baby girl.
But both of them know
the hole that is the missing isn't filled now.
Uhmm, my mother says.
Bless the dead and the living, Grace says.
Then more silence
both of them knowing
there's nothing left to say.

each winter

Each winter
just as the first of the snow begins to fall,
my mother goes home to South Carolina.

Sometimes,

my father goes with her but mostly,
he doesn't.

So she gets on the bus alone.
The first year with one,
the second year with two,
and finally with three children, Hope and Dell hugging
each leg and me
in her arms. Always
there is a fight before she leaves.

Ohio

is where my father wants to be
but to my mother
Ohio will never be home,

no matter
how many plants she brings
indoors each winter, singing softly to them,
the lilt of her words a breath
of warm air moving over each leaf.
In return, they hold on to their color
even as the snow begins to fall. A reminder
of the deep green South. A promise
of life

somewhere.

journey

You can keep your South, my father says.
The way they treated us down there,
I got your mama out as quick as I could.
Brought her right up here to Ohio.

Told her there's never gonna be a Woodson
that sits in the back of the bus.
Never gonna be a Woodson that has to
Yes sir and No sir white people.
Never gonna be a Woodson made to look down
at the ground.

All you kids are stronger than that, my father says.
All you Woodson kids deserve to be
as good as you already are.

Yes sirree, Bob, my father says.
You can keep your South Carolina.

greenville,
south carolina, 1963

On the bus, my mother moves with us to the back.
It is 1963
in South Carolina.
Too dangerous to sit closer to the front
     and dare the driver
to make her move. Not with us. Not now.
Me in her arms all of three months old. My sister
and brother squeezed into the seat beside her. White
shirt, tie, and my brother's head shaved clean.
     My sister's braids
white ribboned.

Sit up straight, my mother says.
She tells my brother to take his fingers
     out of his mouth.
They do what is asked of them.
Although they don't know why they have to.
This isn't Ohio, my mother says,
     as though we understand.
Her mouth a small lipsticked dash, her back

sharp as a line. DO NOT CROSS!
COLOREDS TO THE BACK!
Step off the curb if a white person comes toward you
don't look them in the eye. Yes sir. No sir.
My apologies.
Her eyes straight ahead, my mother
is miles away from here.

Then her mouth softens, her hand moves gently
over my brother's warm head. He is three years old,
his wide eyes open to the world, his too-big ears
already listening. *We're as good as anybody,*
my mother whispers.

As good as anybody.

home

Soon . . .

We are near my other grandparents' house,
    small red stone,
immense yard surrounding it.
Hall Street.
A front porch swing thirsty for oil.
A pot of azaleas blooming.
A pine tree.
Red dirt wafting up
around my mother's newly polished shoes.

Welcome home, my grandparents say.
    Their warm brown
arms around us. A white handkerchief,
    embroidered with blue
to wipe away my mother's tears. And me,
the new baby, set deep
inside this love.

the cousins

It's my mother's birthday and the music
is turned up loud.

Her cousins all around her—the way it was
    before she left.
The same cousins she played with as a girl.
Remember the time, they ask,

When we stole Miz Carter's peach pie off her windowsill,
got stuck in that ditch down below Todd's house,
climbed that fence and snuck into Greenville pool,
weren't scared about getting arrested either, shoot!
nobody telling us where we can and can't swim!

And she laughs, remembering it all.

On the radio, Sam Cooke is singing
    "Twistin' the Night Away":

    Let me tell you 'bout a place
    Somewhere up-a New York way

The cousins have come from as far away as Spartanburg
the boys dressed in skinny-legged pants,
the girls in flowy skirts that swirl out, when they spin
twisting the night away.
Cousin Dorothy's fiancé, holding tight to her hand
    as they twist
Cousin Sam dancing with Mama, ready to catch her
    if she falls, he says
and my mother remembers being a little girl,
    looking down
scared from a high-up tree
and seeing her cousin there—waiting.

Here they have a lot of fun
Puttin' trouble on the run
Twistin' the night away.

I knew you weren't staying up North, the cousins say.
You belong here with us.
My mother throws her head back,
    her newly pressed and curled hair gleaming
her smile the same one she had
    before she left for Columbus.
She's MaryAnn Irby again. Georgiana and Gunnar's
    youngest daughter.

She's home.

night bus

My father arrives on a night bus, his hat in his hands.
It is May now and the rain is coming down.
   Later with the end of this rain
will come the sweet smell of honeysuckle but for now,
there is only the sky opening and my father's tears.
I'm sorry, he whispers.

This fight is over for now.

Tomorrow, we will travel as a family
back to Columbus, Ohio,
Hope and Dell fighting for a place
on my father's lap. Greenville
with its separate ways growing small
behind us.

For now, my parents stand hugging
   in the warm Carolina rain.

No past.

No future.

Just this perfect Now.

after greenville #1

After the chicken is fried and wrapped in wax paper,
tucked gently into cardboard shoe boxes
    and tied with string . . .

After the corn bread is cut into wedges, the peaches
washed and dried . . .

After the sweet tea is poured into mason jars
    twisted tight
and the deviled eggs are scooped back inside
    their egg-white beds
slipped into porcelain bowls that are my mother's now,
    a gift
her mother sends with her on the journey . . .

After the clothes are folded back into suitcases,
the hair ribbons and shirts washed and ironed . . .

After my mother's lipstick is on and my father's
scratchy beginnings of a beard are gone . . .

After our faces are coated
with a thin layer of Vaseline gently wiped off again
with a cool, wet cloth . . .

then it is time to say our good-byes,
   the small clutch of us children
pressed against my grandmother's apron, her tears
quickly blinked away . . .

After the night falls and it is safe
   for brown people to leave
the South without getting stopped
and sometimes beaten
and always questioned:

Are you one of those Freedom Riders?
Are you one of those Civil Rights People?
What gives you the right . . . ?

We board the Greyhound bus, bound
for Ohio.

rivers

The Hocking River moves like a flowing arm away
from the Ohio River
runs through towns as though
it's chasing its own freedom, the same way
the Ohio runs north from Virginia until
it's safely away
from the South.

Each town the Hocking touches tells a story:
Athens
Coolville
Lancaster
Nelsonville,
each
waits for the Hocking water to wash through. Then

as though the river remembers where it belongs
    and what it belongs to,
it circles back, joins up with
    the Ohio again
    as if to say,

I'm sorry.
   as if to say,
I went away from here
but now
   I'm home again.

leaving columbus

When my parents fight for the final time,
my older brother is four,
my sister is nearly three,
and I have just celebrated my first birthday

without celebration.

There is only one photograph of them
    from their time together
a wedding picture, torn from a local newspaper
him in a suit and tie,
her in a bride gown, beautiful
although neither one
is smiling.

Only one photograph.

Maybe the memory of Columbus was too much
for my mother to save
anymore.
Maybe the memory of my mother
was a painful stone inside my father's heart.

But what did it look like
when she finally left him?

A woman nearly six feet tall, straight-backed
and proud, heading down
a cold Columbus street, two small children
beside her and a still-crawling baby
in her arms.

My father, whose reddish-brown skin
would later remind me
of the red dirt of the South
and all that was rich about it, standing
in the yard, one hand
on the black metal railing, the other lifting
into a weak wave good-bye.

As though we were simply guests
leaving Sunday supper.

the
stories
of
south carolina
run
like rivers

PART II

our names

In South Carolina, we become
The Grandchildren
Gunnar's Three Little Ones
Sister Irby's Grands
MaryAnn's Babies

And when we are called by our names
my grandmother
makes them all one
HopeDellJackie
but my grandfather
takes his sweet time, saying each
as if he has all day long

or a whole lifetime.

ohio behind us

When we ask our mother how long we'll be here,
sometimes she says *for a while* and sometimes
she tells us not to ask anymore
because she doesn't know how long we'll stay
in the house where she grew up
on the land she's always known.

When we ask, she tells us
this is where she used to belong
but her sister, Caroline, our aunt Kay, has moved
to the North,
her brother Odell is dead now,
and her baby brother, Robert, says he's almost saved
enough money to follow Caroline to New York City.

Maybe I should go there, too, my mother says.
Everyone else, she says,
has a new place to be now.

Everyone else
has gone away.

And now coming back home
isn't really coming back home
at all.

the garden

Each spring
the dark Nicholtown dirt is filled
with the promise
of what the earth can give back to you
if you work the land
plant the seeds
pull the weeds.

My southern grandfather missed slavery
by one generation. His grandfather
had been owned.
His father worked
the land from dawn till dusk
for the promise of cotton
and a little pay.

So this is what he believes in
your hands in the cool dirt
until the earth gives back to you
all that you've asked of it.

Sweet peas and collards,
green peppers and cukes
lettuce and melon,

berries and peaches and one day
when I'm able, my grandfather says,
I'm gonna figure out how to grow myself a pecan tree.

God gives you what you need, my grandmother says.
Best not to ask for more than that.

Hmph, my grandfather says. And goes back
to working the land, pulling from it all we need

and more than that.

gunnar's children

At dusk, just as the fireflies flicker on, my grandfather
makes his way
home.
We see him coming slow down the road,
his silver lunch box bouncing
soft against his leg. Now,
as he gets closer, we hear him
singing:

"Where will the wedding supper be?
Way down yonder in a hollow tree. Uh hmmm . . ."

Good evening, Miz Clara. Evening, Miz Mae.
How's that leg, Miz Bell?
What you cooking, Auntie Charlotte, you thinking
of making me something to eat?
His voice ringing down Hall Street, circling
round the roads of Nicholtown
and maybe out into the big, wide world . . .

Maybe all the way up in New York,
Aunt Kay's hearing it,
and thinking about coming on home . . .

Then he is close enough to run to—the three of us
climbing him like a tree until he laughs out loud.

We call him Daddy.
This is what our mother calls him.
This is all we know now.

Our daddy seems taller than anyone else
in all of Greenville.
More handsome, too—
His square jaw and light brown eyes
so different from our own
narrow-faced, dark-eyed selves. Still,
his hand is warm and strong around my own
    as I skip beside him,
the wind blowing up around us. He says,
Y'all are Gunnar's children.
Just keep remembering that.

Just keep remembering . . .

This is the way of Nicholtown evenings,
Daddy
coming home,

me
jumping into his arms,
the others

circling around him
all of us grinning
all of us talking
all of us loving him up.

at the end of the day

There are white men working at the printing press
beside Daddy, their fingers blackened
with ink so that at the end of the day, palms up
it's hard to tell who is white and who is not, still
they call my grandfather Gunnar,
even though he's a foreman
and is supposed to be called
Mr. Irby.
But he looks the white men in the eye
sees the way so many of them can't understand
a colored man
telling them what they need to do.
This is new. Too fast for them.
The South is changing.

Sometimes they don't listen.
Sometimes they walk away.
At the end of the day, the newspaper is printed,
the machines are shut down and each man
punches a clock and leaves but

only Colored folks
come home to Nicholtown.

Here, you can't look right or left or up or down
without seeing brown people.
Colored Town. Brown Town. Even a few mean words
to say where we live.

My grandmother tells us
it's the way of the South. *Colored folks used to stay*
where they were told that they belonged. But
times are changing.
And people are itching to go where they want.

This evening, though,
I am happy to belong
to Nicholtown.

daywork

There is daywork for colored women.
In the mornings their dark bodies
fill the crosstown buses,
taking them away
from Nicholtown
to the other side
of Greenville
where the white people live.
Our grandmother tells us this
as she sets a small hat with a topaz pin on her head,
pulls white gloves
over her soft brown hands.
Two days a week, she joins the women,
taking on this second job now
that there are four more mouths to feed
and the money
she gets from part-time teaching isn't enough
anymore. *I'm not ashamed,* she says,
cleaning is what I know. I'm not ashamed,
if it feeds my children.

When she returns in the evening, her hands
are ashen from washing other people's clothes,
Most often by hand,
her ankles swollen from standing all day
making beds and sweeping floors,
shaking dust from curtains,
picking up after other people's children, cooking,
the list
goes on and on.
Don't any of you ever do daywork, she warns us.
I'm doing it now so you don't have to.
And maybe all across Nicholtown, other children
are hearing this, too.

Get the Epsom salts, she says, leaning back
into the soft brown chair, her eyes closing.
When she isn't in it, Hope, Dell and I squeeze in
side by side by side and still, there is space left
for one more.
We fill a dishpan with warm water, pour
the salts in, swirl it around and carefully
carry it to her feet. We fight to see who will get
to rub the swelling from my grandmother's ankles,
the smile back onto her face,
the stories back into the too-quiet room.

*You could have eaten off the floor by the time
I left this one house today,*

my grandmother begins, letting out a heavy sigh. *But
let me tell you,
when I first got there, you would have thought
the Devil himself had come through . . .*

lullaby

At night, every living thing competes
for a chance to be heard.
The crickets
and frogs call out.
Sometimes, there's the soft
who-whoo of an owl lost
amid the pines.
Even the dogs won't rest until
they've howled
at the moon.

But the crickets always win, long after
the frogs stop croaking
and the owl has found its way home.
Long after the dogs have lain down
losing the battle against sleep,
the crickets keep going
as though they know their song
is our lullaby.

bible times

My grandmother keeps her Bible on a shelf
beside her bed. When the day is over,
she reads quietly to herself, and in the morning
she'll tell us the stories,
how Noah listened
to God's word
pulled two of each animal inside his ark, waited
for the rains to come and floated safely
as the sinners drowned.

It's morning now and we have floated safely
through the Nicholtown night,
our evening prayers
Jehovah, please give us another day,
now answered.
Biscuits warm and buttered stop halfway
to our mouths. *How much rain did it take
to destroy the sinners? What lies did they tell
to die such a death? How loud was the rain
when it came? How did Noah know
that the cobra wouldn't bite, the bull
wouldn't charge, the bee wouldn't sting?*

Our questions come fast but we want
the stories more than we want the answers
so when my grandmother says,
Hush, so I can tell it!
We do.
Jacob's dream of a ladder to heaven, and Jesus
with the children surrounding him. Moses
on the mountain, fire burning words into stone.
Even Salome intrigues us, her wish for a man's head
on a platter—who could want this and live
to tell the story of that wanting?

Autumn is coming.
Outside, there's the sound of wind
through the pine trees.
But inside there are stories, there are biscuits
and grits and eggs, the fire in the potbellied stove
already filling the house with warmth.

Still we shiver at the thought of evil Salome,
chew our biscuits slowly.
We are safe here—miles and years away
from Bible Times.

the reader

When we can't find my sister, we know
she is under the kitchen table, a book in her hand,
a glass of milk and a small bowl of peanuts beside her.

We know we can call Odella's name out loud,
slap the table hard with our hands,
dance around it singing
"She'll Be Coming 'Round the Mountain"
so many times the song makes us sick
and the circling makes us dizzy
and still
my sister will do nothing more
than slowly turn the page.

the beginning

I cannot write a word yet but at three,
I now know the letter *J*
love the way it curves into a hook
that I carefully top with a straight hat
the way my sister has taught me to do. Love
the sound of the letter and the promise
that one day this will be connected to a full name,

my own

that I will be able to write

by myself.

Without my sister's hand over mine,
making it do what I cannot yet do.

How amazing these words are that slowly come to me.
How wonderfully on and on they go.

Will the words end, I ask
whenever I remember to.

Nope, my sister says, all of five years old now,
and promising me

infinity.

hope

The South doesn't agree
with my brother.
The heat sandpapers his skin.
Don't scratch, my grandmother warns. But he does
and the skin grows raw beneath his fingers.
The pollen leaves him puffy eyed, his small breaths
come quick, have too much sound around them.
He moves slow, sickly now where once
he was strong.
And when his body isn't betraying him, Ohio does.
The memories waking him in the night, the view
from my father's shoulders, the wonder
of the Nelsonville house, the air
so easy to breathe . . .

You can keep your South, my father had said.

Now Hope stays mostly quiet
unless asked to speak, his head bent
inside the superhero comic books my grandfather
brings home on Fridays. Hope searches for himself
inside their pages. Leaves them
dog-eared by Monday morning.

The South
his mortal enemy.
The South,
his Kryptonite.

the almost friends

There's the boy from up the road
with the hole in his heart. Some afternoons
he comes to sit in our yard and listen
to our stories. Our aunt Kay, we tell him,
lives in New York City and maybe we will, too,
someday. And yes it's true, once
we lived in Ohio, that's why
we speak the way we do.
We don't ask about the hole
in his heart. Our grandmother warns us
we know better than that.

There is Cora and her sisters, across the road.
One word in my grandmother's mouth—*You stay away
from Coraandhersisters,* their mother
left the family, ran off
with their church pastor.
Coraandhersisters
sometimes
sit watching us.
We watch them back not asking
what it feels like not to have a mother because

our grandmother warns us
we know better than that.

There are three brothers who live down the road
we know this only because
our grandmother tells us. They live
inside their dark house
all summer, coming out
in the evening when their mother returns from work
long after we've bathed and slipped into
our summer pajamas, books curled into
our arms.

These are our almost friends, the people
we think about when we're tired of playing
with each other.

But our grandmother says,
Three is plenty. Three is a team.
Find something to do together.
And so over and over again,
we do. Even though we want to ask her,
Why can't we play with them? we don't.

We know better than that.

the right way
to speak

The first time my brother says *ain't* my mother
pulls a branch from the willow tree growing down
the hill at the edge
of our backyard.
As she slips her closed hand over it,
removing the leaves,
my brother begins to cry
because the branch is a switch now

no longer beautifully weeping at the bottom of the hill.
It whirs as my mother whips it
through the air and down
against my brother's legs.

You will never, my mother says,
say ain't in this house.
You will never
say ain't anywhere.

Each switching is a warning to us
our words are to remain

crisp and clear.
We are never to say *huh?*
ain't or *y'all*
git or *gonna.*
Never *ma'am*—just *yes,* with eyes
meeting eyes enough
to show respect.
Don't ever ma'am anyone!
The word too painful
a memory for my mother
of not-so-long-ago
southern subservient days . . .

The list of what not to say
goes on and on . . .

You are from the North, our mother says.
You know the right way to speak.

As the switch raises dark welts on my brother's legs
Dell and I look on
afraid to open our mouths. Fearing the South
will slip out or
into them.

the candy lady

On Fridays, our grandfather takes us
to the candy lady's house,
even though our grandmother worries he's going
to be the cause of our teeth rotting
right out of our heads.
But my grandfather just laughs,
makes us open our mouths
to show the strong Irby teeth we've inherited
from *his* side of the family.
The three of us stand there, our mouths open wide,
strong white teeth inside,
and my grandmother has to nod, has to say,
They're lucky before sending us on our way.

The candy lady's small living room is filled
with shelves and shelves of chocolate bars
and gumdrops, Good & Plenty and Jujubes,
Moon Pies and Necco Wafers,
lollipops and long red licorice strings.
So much candy that it's hard to choose
until our grandfather says,
Get what you want but I'm getting myself some ice cream.

Then the candy lady, who is gray-haired
and never smiles, disappears
into another room and returns a few minutes later
with a wafer cone, pale yellow
lemon-chiffon ice cream dripping from it.
Outside, even this late in the afternoon,
the sun is beating down
and the idea of lemon-chiffon ice cream cooling us,
even for a few minutes,
makes us all start saying at once—*Me, too, Daddy.*
Me, too, Daddy. Me, too.

The walk home from the candy lady's house
is a quiet one
except for the sound of melting ice cream
being slurped up
fast, before it slides past our wrists,
on down our arms and onto
the hot, dry road.

south carolina at war

Because we have a right, my grandfather tells us—
we are sitting at his feet and the story tonight is

why people are marching all over the South—

to walk and sit and dream wherever we want.

First they brought us here.
Then we worked for free. Then it was 1863,
and we were supposed to be free but we weren't.

And that's why people are so mad.

And it's true, we can't turn on the radio
without hearing about the marching.

We can't go to downtown Greenville without
seeing the teenagers walking into stores, sitting
where brown people still aren't allowed to sit
and getting carried out, their bodies limp,
     their faces calm.

This is the way brown people have to fight,
my grandfather says.
You can't just put your fist up. You have to insist
on something
gently. Walk toward a thing
slowly.

But be ready to die,
my grandfather says,
for what is right.

Be ready to die, my grandfather says,
for everything you believe in.

And none of us can imagine death
but we try to imagine it anyway.

Even my mother joins the fight.
When she thinks our grandmother
isn't watching she sneaks out
to meet the cousins downtown, but just as
    she's stepping through the door,
her good dress and gloves on, my grandmother says,
Now don't go getting arrested.

And Mama sounds like a little girl when she says,
I won't.

More than a hundred years, my grandfather says,
and we're still fighting for the free life
we're supposed to be living.

So there's a war going on in South Carolina
and even as we play
and plant and preach and sleep, we are a part of it.

Because you're colored, my grandfather says.
And just as good and bright and beautiful and free
as anybody.
And nobody colored in the South is stopping,
my grandfather says,
until everybody knows what's true.

the training

When my mother's older cousin
and best friend, Dorothy,
comes with her children, they run off
saying they can't understand
the way Hope, Dell and I speak.
Y'all go too fast, they say.
And the words get all pushed together.
They say they don't feel like playing
with us little kids. So they leave us
to walk the streets of Nicholtown when we can't
leave the porch.
We watch them go, hear
Cousin Dorothy say, *Don't you knuckleheads*
get into trouble out there.
Then we stay close to Cousin Dorothy, make believe
we're not listening when she knows we are.
Laughing when she laughs, shaking our own heads
when she shakes
hers. *You know how you have to get those trainings,*
she says, and our mother nods. *They*
won't let you sit at the counters

without them. Have to know what to do
when those people come at you.
She has a small space between her teeth
like my mother's space, and Hope's and Dell's, too.
She is tall and dark-skinned,
beautiful and broad shouldered.
She wears gloves and dark-colored dresses made for her
by a seamstress in Charleston.

The trainings take place in the basements of churches
and the back rooms of stores,
on long car trips and anywhere else where people can
gather. They learn
how to change the South without violence,
how to not be moved
by the evil actions of others, how to walk slowly but
with deliberate steps.
How to sit at counters and be cursed at
without cursing back, have food and drinks poured
over them without standing up and hurting someone.
Even the teenagers
get trained to sit tall, not cry, swallow back fear.

But Lord, Cousin Dorothy says. *Everybody has a line.*
When I'm walking
up to that lunch counter and taking my seat,
I pray to God, don't let

anybody spit on me. I can be Sweet Dorothy
seven days a week, twenty-four hours a day
as long as nobody crosses that line. Because if they do,
this nonviolent movement

is over!

the blanket

The first time my mother goes to New York City
it is only for a long-weekend visit,
her kiss on our cheeks
as much a promise as the excitement in her eyes.
I'll bring something back for each of you.

It's Friday night and the weekend ahead
is already calling us
to the candy lady's house,
my hand in Daddy's.
He doesn't know how to say no,
my grandmother complains.

But neither does she,
dresses and socks and ribbons,
our hair pressed and curled.
She calls my sister and me her baby girls,
smiles proudly when the women say how pretty we are.

So the first time my mother goes to New York City
we don't know to be sad, the weight

of our grandparents' love like a blanket
with us beneath it,
safe and warm.

miss bell and
the marchers

They look like regular people
visiting our neighbor Miss Bell,
foil-covered dishes held out in front of them
as they arrive
some in pairs,
some alone,
some just little kids
holding their mothers' hands.

If you didn't know, you'd think it was just
an evening gathering. Maybe church people
heading into Miss Bell's house to talk
about God. But when Miss Bell pulls her blinds
closed, the people fill their dinner plates with food,
their glasses with sweet tea and gather
to talk about marching.

And even though Miss Bell works for a white lady
who said *I will fire you in a minute if I ever see you
on that line!*
Miss Bell knows that marching isn't the only thing

she can do,
knows that people fighting need full bellies to think
and safe places to gather.
She knows the white lady isn't the only one
who's watching, listening, waiting,
to end this fight. So she keeps the marchers'
glasses filled, adds more corn bread
and potato salad to their plates,
stands in the kitchen ready to slice
lemon pound cake into generous pieces.

And in the morning, just before she pulls
her uniform from the closet, she prays,
*God, please give me and those people marching
another day.*

Amen.

how to listen #2

In the stores downtown
we're always followed around
just because we're brown.

hair night

Saturday night smells of biscuits and burning hair.
Supper done and my grandmother has transformed
the kitchen into a beauty shop. Laid across the table
is the hot comb, Dixie Peach hair grease,
horsehair brush, parting stick
and one girl at a time.
Jackie first, my sister says,
our freshly washed hair damp
and spiraling over toweled shoulders
and pale cotton nightgowns.
She opens her book to the marked page,
curls up in a chair pulled close
to the wood-burning stove, bowl of peanuts in her lap.
The words
in her books are so small, I have to squint
to see the letters. *Hans Brinker or The Silver Skates.*
The House at Pooh Corner. Swiss Family Robinson.
Thick books
dog-eared from the handing down from neighbor
to neighbor. My sister handles them gently,
marks the pages with torn brown pieces
of paper bag, wipes her hands before going

beyond the hardbound covers.
Read to me, I say, my eyes and scalp already stinging
from the tug of the brush through my hair.
And while my grandmother sets the hot comb
on the flame, heats it just enough to pull
my tight curls straighter, my sister's voice
wafts over the kitchen,
past the smell of hair and oil and flame, settles
like a hand on my shoulder and holds me there.
I want silver skates like Hans's, a place
on a desert island. I have never seen the ocean
but this, too, I can imagine—blue water pouring
over red dirt.
As my sister reads, the pictures begin forming
as though someone has turned on a television,
lowered the sound,
pulled it up close.
Grainy black-and-white pictures come slowly at me
Deep. Infinite. Remembered

On a bright December morning long ago . . .

My sister's clear soft voice opens up the world to me.
I lean in
so hungry for it.

Hold still now, my grandmother warns.
So I sit on my hands to keep my mind

off my hurting head, and my whole body still.
But the rest of me is already leaving,
the rest of me is already gone.

family names

There's James, Joseph, Andrew, Geneva, Annie Mae,
William, Lucinda, David, Talmudge,
my grandmother says. All together,
my mama gave birth to thirteen children.
Our heads spin at the thought of that many brothers
and sisters. Three died as babies, she says,
but only a little of the spinning stops.

There's Levonia, Montague, Iellus, Hallique,
Valie Mae, Virdie and Elora on my daddy's side.
We can't help but laugh each time our daddy
tells us the names of his brothers and sisters.
His own name,
Gunnar, sends us laughing all over again.
Gave their kids names
that no master could ever take away.
What about Bob or Joe? Hope wants to know.
What about
John or Michael? Or something real normal, like Hope?
Hope is not normal, my sister says. Not for a boy. I think
your name is a mistake. Maybe they meant
to name you Virdie.

I'm the great Hope of the family, my brother says.
Just like Grandpa Hope.
Just like Hope the Dope, my sister says back.

Keep up the arguing, my grandfather says,
I'll take you both down to city hall.
People be happy to call you Talmudge and Valie Mae.

american dream

Even when my girls were little, we'd go down there,
my grandmother tells us. *And people'd be marching.*
The marching didn't just start yesterday.
Police with those dogs, scared everybody
near to death. Just once
I let my girls march.

My grandmother leans back in her brown chair,
her feet still in the Epsom salts water,
her fingers tapping out
some silent tune. She closes her eyes.
I let them and I prayed.

What's the thing, I ask her, *that would make people*
want to live together?

People have to want it, that's all.

We get quiet—maybe all of us are thinking about
the ones who want it. And the ones who don't.

We all have the same dream, my grandmother says.
To live equal in a country that's supposed to be
the land of the free.
She lets out a long breath,
deep remembering.

When your mother was little
she wanted a dog. But I said no.
Quick as you can blink, I told her,
a dog will turn on you.

So my mother brought kittens home,
soft and purring inside of empty boxes
mewing and mewing until my grandmother
fell in love. And let her keep them.

My grandmother tells us all this
as we sit at her feet, each story like a photograph
we can look right into, see our mother there
marchers and dogs and kittens all blending
and us now
there in each moment
beside her.

the fabric store

Some Fridays, we walk to downtown Greenville where
there are some clothing stores, some restaurants,
a motel and the five-and-dime store but
my grandmother won't take us
into any of those places anymore.
Even the five-and-dime, which isn't segregated now
but where a woman is paid, my grandmother says,
to follow colored people around in case they try to
steal something. We don't go into the restaurants
because they always seat us near the kitchen.
When we go downtown,
we go to the fabric store, where the white woman
knows my grandmother
from back in Anderson, asks,
How's Gunnar doing and your girls in New York?
She rolls fabric out for my grandmother
to rub between her fingers.
They discuss drape and nap and where to cinch
the waist on a skirt for a child.
At the fabric store, we are not Colored

or Negro. We are not thieves or shameful
or something to be hidden away.
At the fabric store, we're just people.

ghosts

In downtown Greenville,
they painted over the WHITE ONLY signs,
except on the bathroom doors,
they didn't use a lot of paint
so you can still see the words, right there
like a ghost standing in front
still keeping you out.

the leavers

We watch men leave Greenville
in their one good suit, shoes
spit shined.
We watch women leave in Sunday clothes,
hatted and lipsticked and white gloved.

We watch them catch buses in the evening,
the black shadows of their backs
the last we see of them.
Others fill their cars with bags.
Whole families disappearing into the night.
People waving good-bye.

They say the City is a place where diamonds
speckle the sidewalk. Money
falls from the sky.
They say a colored person can do well going there.
All you need is the fare out of Greenville.
All you need is to know somebody on the other side,
waiting to cross you over.

Like the River Jordan

and then you're in Paradise.

the beginning of the leaving

When my mother returns from New York
she has a new plan—all of us are going
to move there. We don't know
anyplace else but Greenville now—New York
is only the pictures she shows us
in magazines and the two she has in her pocketbook
of our aunt Kay. In one, there are two other people
   standing with her.
Bernie and Peaches, our mother tells us.
   We all used to be friends
here in Nicholtown.
That's all the young kids used to talk about,
our grandmother tells us,
going to New York City.

My mother smiles at us and says,
We'll be going to New York City.
I just have to figure some things out first, that's all.

I don't know what I'd do without you all up under me,
my grandmother says and there's a sadness
in her voice.
Don't know what I'd do, she says again.
Even sadder this time.

as a child, i smelled the air

Mama takes her coffee out to the front porch
sips it slow. Two steps down and her feet
are covered in grass and dew.
New York doesn't smell like this, she says.

I follow her, the dew cool against my feet
the soft hush of wind through leaves
my mother and I
alone together.

Her coffee is sweetened with condensed milk,
her hair pulled back into a braid,
her dark fingers circling her cup.
If I ask, she will hold it to my lips,
let me taste the bittersweet of it.

It's dawn and the birds have come alive, chasing
each other from maple to pine and back
to maple again. This is how time passes here.
The maple will be bare-branched come winter,
Mama says. *But the pines, they just keep on living.*

And the air is what I'll remember.
Even once we move to New York.

It always smelled like this, my mother says.
Wet grass and pine.

Like memory.

harvest time

When Daddy's garden is ready
it is filled with words that make me laugh
when I say them—
pole beans and *tomatoes, okra* and *corn*
sweet peas and *sugar snaps,*
lettuce and *squash.*

Who could have imagined

so much color that the ground disappears
and we are left
walking through an autumn's worth
of crazy words
that beneath the magic
of my grandmother's hands

become

side dishes.

grown folks' stories

Warm autumn night with the crickets crying
the smell of pine coming soft on the wind
and the women
on the porch, quilts across their laps,
Aunt Lucinda, Miss Bell and whatever neighbor
has a *breath or two left* at the end of the day
for *sitting and running our mouths.*

That's when we listen
to the grown folks talking.
Hope, Dell and me sitting quiet on the stairs.
We know one word from us will bring a hush
upon the women, my grandmother's finger suddenly
pointing toward the house, her soft-spoken
I think it's time for you kids to go to bed now ushering
us into our room. So we are silent, our backs against
posts and the back of the stairs, Hope's elbows
on his knees, head down. Now is when we learn
everything
there is to know
about the people down the road and
in the daywork houses,

about the Sisters at the Kingdom Hall
and the faraway relatives we rarely see.

Long after the stories are told, I remember them,
whisper them back to Hope
and Dell late into the night:
She's the one who left Nicholtown in the daytime
the one Grandmama says wasn't afraid
of anything. Retelling each story.
Making up what I didn't understand
or missed when voices dropped too low, I talk
until my sister and brother's soft breaths tell me
they've fallen
asleep.

Then I let the stories live
inside my head, again and again
until the real world fades back
into cricket lullabies
and my own dreams.

tobacco

Summer is over, a kiss
of chill in the southern air. We see the dim orange
of my grandfather's cigarette, as he makes his way
down the darkening road. Hear his evening greetings
and the coughing that follows them.
Not enough breath left now
to sing so I sing for him, in my head
where only I can hear.

Where will the wedding supper be?
Way down yonder in a hollow tree. Uh hmmm . . .

The old people used to say
a pinch of dirt in the mouth
can tell tobacco's story:
what crops
are ready for picking
what needs to be left to grow.
What soil is rich enough for planting
and the patches of land that need
a year of rest.

I do not know yet
how sometimes the earth makes a promise
it can never keep. Tobacco fields
lay fallow, crops picked clean.
My grandfather coughs again
and the earth waits

for what and who it will get in return.

how to listen #3

Middle of the night
my grandfather is coughing
me upright. Startled.

my mother
leaving greenville

It is late autumn now, the smell of wood burning,
the potbellied stove like a warm soft hand
in the center of my grandparents' living room,
its black pipe
stretching into the ceiling then disappearing.

So many years have passed since we last saw
our father, his absence
like a bubble in my older brother's life,
that pops again and again
into a whole lot of tiny bubbles
of memory.

You were just a baby, he says to me.
*You're so lucky you don't remember the fighting
or anything.*

It's like erasers came through her memory, my sister says.
Erase. Erase. Erase.

But now, my mother is leaving again.

This, I will remember.

halfway home #1

New York, my mother says.
Soon, I'll find us a place there. Come back
and bring you all home.

She wants a place of her own that is not
The Nelsonville House, The Columbus House,
The Greenville House.
Looking for her next place.
Our next place.
Right now, our mother says,
we're only halfway home.

And I imagine her standing
in the middle of a road, her arms out
fingers pointing North and South.

I want to ask:
Will there always be a road?
Will there always be a bus?
Will we always have to choose
between home

and home?

my mother looks back
on greenville

After our dinner and bath,
after our powdered and pajamaed bodies are tucked
three across into bed,
after *Winnie the Pooh* and kisses on our foreheads
and longer-than-usual hugs,

my mother walks away from the house on Hall Street
out into the growing night,
down a long dusty road
to where the Nicholtown bus
takes her to the Greyhound station

then more dust

then she's gone.

New York ahead of her,
her family behind, she moves
to the back, her purse in her lap,
the land
pulling her gaze to the window once more.
Before darkness
covers it and for many hours, there are only shadows

and stars

and tears

and hope.

the last fireflies

We know our days are counted here.
Each evening we wait for the first light
of the last fireflies, catch them in jars
then let them go again. As though we understand
their need for freedom.
As though our silent prayers to stay in Greenville
will be answered if
we do what we know is right.

changes

Now the evenings are quiet with my mother gone
as though the night is listening
to the way we are counting the days. We know
even the feel of our grandmother's brush
being pulled gently through our hair
will fast become a memory. Those Saturday evenings
at her kitchen table, the smell
of Dixie Peach hair grease,
the sizzle of the straightening comb,
the hiss of the iron
against damp, newly washed ribbons, all of this
may happen again, but in another place.

We sit on our grandparents' porch,
shivering already against the coming winter,
and talk softly about Greenville summer,
how when we come back,
we'll do all the stuff we always did,
hear the same stories,
laugh at the same jokes, catch fireflies in the same
mason jars, promise each other

future summers that are as good as the past.
But we know we are lying

coming home will be different now.

This place called Greenville
this neighborhood called Nicholtown
will change some

and so will each of us.

sterling high school,
greenville

While my mother is away in New York City,
a fire sweeps through
her old high school
during a senior dance.

Smoke filled the crowded room
and the music
stopped
and the students dancing
stopped
and the DJ told them
to quickly leave the building.

The fire
lasted all night
and when it was over,
my mother's high school had burned
nearly to the ground.

My mother said it was because
the students had been marching,

and the marching
made some white people in Greenville mad.

After the fire the students weren't allowed to go to
the all-white high school.
Instead they had to crowd in
beside their younger sisters and brothers
at the lower school.

In the photos from my mother's high school yearbook—
                    The Torch, 1959,
my mother is smiling beside her cousin
Dorothy Ann and on her other side,
there is Jesse Jackson,
who maybe was already dreaming of one day
being the first brown man to run
for president.

And not even
the torching of their school
could stop him or the marchers
from changing the world.

faith

After my mother leaves, my grandmother
pulls us further
into the religion she has always known.
We become Jehovah's Witnesses
like her.

After my mother leaves
there is no one
to say,
The children can choose their own faith
when they're old enough.
In my house, my grandmother says,
you will do as I do.

After my mother leaves,
we wake in the middle of the night
calling out for her.
Have faith, my grandmother says
pulling us to her in the darkness.

Let the Bible,
my grandmother says,
become your sword and your shield.

But we do not know yet
who we are fighting
and what we are fighting for.

the stories cora tells

In the evening now
Coraandhersisters come over to our porch.
There are three of them
and three of us but Hope
moves away from the girls
sits by himself
out in the yard.

And even though my grandmother tells us
not to play with them,
she doesn't call us into the house anymore
when she sees them walking down the road. Maybe
her heart moves over a bit
making room for them.

A colorful mushroom grows
beneath the pine tree. Purple and gold and strange
against the pine-needled ground.
When I step on it,
Coraandhersisters scream at me,
You just killed the Devil while he was sleeping!
Sleeping in his own house.

Cora warns me
the Devil will soon be alive again.
She says, *He's going to come for you,*
late in the night while you're sleeping
and the God y'all pray to won't be there protecting you.

I cry as the sun sets, waiting.
Cry until my grandmother comes out
shoos Coraandhersisters home
holds me tight
tells me they are lying.
That's just some crazy southern superstition,
my grandmother says.
Those girls must be a little simple not knowing
a mushroom when they see one.
Don't believe everything you hear, Jackie.
Someday, you'll come to know
when someone is telling the truth
and when they're just making up stories.

hall street

In the early evening, just before the best light
for hide-and-seek
takes over the sky,
it's Bible-study time. We watch
from our places on the front porch, our cold hands
cupped around hot chocolate
half gone and sweetest at the bottom
as the Brother and Sister
from the Kingdom Hall make their way up our road.

Pretty Monday evening, the Brother
from the Kingdom Hall says.
Thank Jehovah, the Sister
from the Kingdom Hall says back.
We are silent, Brother Hope, Sister Dell and me.

None of us want to sit inside when the late autumn
is calling to us
and frogs are finally feeling brave enough
to hop across our yard. We want
anything but this. We want warm biscuits

and tag and jacks on the porch,
our too-long sweater sleeves
getting in the way sometimes.

But we are Jehovah's Witnesses. Monday night
is Bible-study time.

Somewhere else,
my grandfather is
spending time with his brother Vertie.
Maybe they are playing the harmonica and banjo,
laughing and singing loud. Doing
what's fun to do on a pretty Monday evening.

Jehovah promises us everlasting life in the New World,
the Brother from the Kingdom Hall says
and Brother Hope, Sister Dell and me are silent
wanting only what's right outside.
Wanting only this world.

soon

When the phone rings in my grandmother's kitchen,
we run from wherever we are,
jumping from the front porch swing
climbing out of the mud-filled ditch out back,
running quick from the picked-clean garden—
but
my brother, Hope, is the fastest, picking up the phone,
pressing it hard
against his ear as though my mother's voice
just that much closer means my mother is
closer to us. We jump around him:
Let me speak! until my grandmother comes
through the screen door
puts down the basket of laundry, cold and dry
from the line
takes the phone from my brother,
shushes us,
shoos us,
promises us

a moment with our mother soon.

how i learn
the days of the week

Monday night is Bible study with a Brother and Sister
from the Kingdom Hall.

Tuesday night is Bible study at the Kingdom Hall.

Wednesday night is laundry night—the clothes
blowing clean on the line above
my grandfather's garden. When no one is looking,
we run through the sheets,
breathe in all the wonderful smells the air
   adds to them.

Thursday night is Ministry School. One day,
we will grow up to preach
God's word, take it out
into the world
and maybe we'll save some people.

Friday night, we're free as anything,
Hope and Dell's bikes skidding along Hall Street,
my knees bumping hard against the handlebars

of my red three-wheeler. One more year maybe
Dell's bike will be mine.

Saturday we're up early: *The Watchtower* and *Awake!*
in our hands, we walk like sleepy soldiers
through Nicholtown, ringing bells, knocking on doors,
spreading the good news
of something better coming. Sometimes,
the people listen.
Sometimes, they slam their doors
or don't open them at all. Or look sadly down at me
ribboned and starched, my face clean and shining
with oil, my words earnest as anything:
Good morning, I'm Sister Jacqueline and I'm here
to bring you some good news today.
Sometimes they give me a dime but won't take
my *Watchtower* and *Awake!*

Sunday it's *Watchtower* study at the Kingdom Hall,
two hours
of sitting and sitting and sitting.

Then Monday comes and the week starts
all over again.

ribbons

They are pale blue or pink or white.
They are neatly ironed each Saturday night.
Come Sunday morning, they are tied to the braids
hanging down past our ears.

We wear ribbons every day except Saturday
when we wash them by hand, Dell and I
side by side at the kitchen sink,
rubbing them with Ivory soap then rinsing them
beneath cool water.
Each of us
dreaming of the day our grandmother says
You're too old for ribbons.

But it feels like that day will never come.

When we hang them on the line to dry, we hope
they'll blow away in the night breeze
but they don't. Come morning, they're right
where we left them
gently moving in the cool air, eager to anchor us
to childhood.

two gods.
two worlds

It's barely morning and we're already awake,
my grandmother in the kitchen ironing
our Sunday clothes.

I can hear Daddy coughing in his bed, a cough like
he'll never catch his breath. The sound catches
in my chest as I'm pulling my dress
over my head. Hold my own breath
until the coughing stops. Still,
I hear him pad through the living room
hear the squeak of the front screen door and
know, he's made it to the porch swing,
to smoke a cigarette.

My grandfather doesn't believe in a God
that won't let him smoke
or have a cold beer on a Friday night
a God that tells us all
the world is ending so that *Y'all walk through this world*
afraid as cats.

Your God is not my God, he says.

His cough moves through the air
back into our room where the light
is almost blue, the white winter sun painting it.
I wish the coughing would stop. I wish
he would put on Sunday clothes,
take my hand, walk with us
down the road.

Jehovah's Witnesses believe
that everyone who doesn't follow
God's word will be destroyed in a great battle called
Armageddon. And when the battle is done
there will be a fresh new world
a nicer more peaceful world.

But I want the world where my daddy is
and don't know why
anybody's God would make me
have to choose.

what god knows

We pray for my grandfather
ask God to spare him even though
he's a nonbeliever. We ask that Jehovah look
into his heart, see
the goodness there.

But my grandfather says he doesn't need our prayers.
I work hard, he says. *I treat people like I want
to be treated.*
God sees this. God knows.

At the end of the day
he lights a cigarette, unlaces
his dusty brogans. Stretches his legs.
God sees my good, he says.
*Do all the preaching and praying you want
but no need to do it for me.*

new playmates

Beautiful brown dolls come from New York City,
fancy stores my mother has walked
into. She writes of elevators, train stations,
buildings so high, they hurt
the neck to see.

She writes of places with beautiful names
Coney Island, Harlem, Brownsville, Bear Mountain.
She tells us she's seen the ocean, how the water
keeps going long after the eyes can't see it anymore
promises a whole other country
on the other side.

She tells us the toy stores are filled with dolls
    of every size and color
there's a barbershop and a hair salon everywhere
    you look
and a friend of Aunt Kay's saw Lena Horne
just walking down the street.

But only the dolls are real to us.

Their black hair in stiff curls down

over their shoulders,
their pink dresses made of crinoline and satin.
Their dark arms unbending.
Still
we hug their hard plastic close and imagine
they're calling us Mama
imagine they need us near.
Imagine the letters from our own mother—
Coming to get you soon—
are ones we're writing to them.
We will never leave you, we whisper.
They stare back at us,
blank-eyed and beautiful
silent and still.

down the road

Be careful when you play with him,
my grandmother warns us about the boy
with the hole in his heart.
Don't make him run too fast. Or cry.

When he taps on our back door, we come out
sit quietly with him on the back stairs.
He doesn't talk much, this boy with the hole
in his heart
but when he does, it's to ask us about our mother
in New York City.

Is she afraid there?
Did she ever meet a movie star?
Do the buildings really
go on and on?

One day, he says—so soft, my brother, sister and I
lean in to hear—*I'm gonna go to New York City.*
Then he looks off, toward Cora's house down the road.

That's south, my sister says. *New York's the other way.*

god's promise

It is nearly Christmastime.
On the radio, a man with a soft deep voice is singing
telling us to have ourselves a merry little . . .

Nicholtown windows are filled with Christmas trees.
Coraandhersisters brag about what they are getting,
dolls and skates and swing sets. In the backyard
our own swing set is silent—
a thin layer of snow covering it.
When we are made to stay inside on Sunday
afternoons,
Coraandhersisters descend upon it, take the swings
up high,
stick their tongues out at us
as we stare from behind our glassed-in screen door.

Let them play, for heaven's sake, my grandmother says,
when we complain about them tearing it apart.
Your hearts are bigger than that!

But our hearts aren't bigger than that.
Our hearts are tiny and mad.
If our hearts were hands, they'd hit.
If our hearts were feet, they'd surely kick somebody!

the other infinity

We are the chosen people, our grandmother tells us.
*Everything we do is a part
of God's plan. Every breath you breathe is the gift God
is giving you. Everything we own . . .*

Daddy gave us the swings, my sister tells her. *Not God.*

My grandmother's words come slowly meaning
this lesson is an important one.

*With the money he earned by working at a job God
gave him a body strong enough to work with.*

Outside, our swing set is empty finally,
Coraandhersisters now gone.

Hope, Dell and I are silent.
So much we don't yet understand.
So much we don't yet believe.

But we know this:
Monday, Tuesday, Thursday,
Saturday and Sunday are reserved
for God's work. We are put here to do it

and we are expected to do it well.
What is promised to us in return

is eternity.

It's the same, my sister says,
or maybe even better than
infinity.

The empty swing set reminds us of this—
that what is bad won't be bad forever,
and what is good can sometimes last
a long, long time.

Even Coraandhersisters can only bother us
for a little while before they get called home
to supper.

sometimes,
no words are needed

Deep winter and the night air is cold. So still,
it feels like the world goes on forever in the darkness
until you look up and the earth stops
in a ceiling of stars. My head against
my grandfather's arm,
a blanket around us as we sit on the front porch swing.
Its whine like a song.

You don't need words
on a night like this. Just the warmth
of your grandfather's arm. Just the silent promise
that the world as we know it
will always be here.

the letter

The letter comes on a Saturday morning,
my sister opens it. My mother's handwriting
is easy, my sister says. *She doesn't write in script.*
She writes so we can understand her.

And then she reads my mother's letter slowly
while Hope and I sit at the kitchen table,
cheese grits near gone, scrambled eggs
leaving yellow dots
in our bowls. My grandmother's beloved biscuits
forgotten.
She's coming for us, my sister says and reads the part
where my mother tells her the plan.
We're really leaving Greenville, my sister says
and Hope sits up straighter
and smiles. But then the smile is gone.
How can we have both places?
How can we leave
all that we've known—
me on Daddy's lap in the early evening,
listening to Hope and Dell tell stories

about their lives at the small school
a mile down the road.
I will be five one day and the Nicholtown school
is a mystery
I'm just about to solve.

And what about the fireflies and ditches?
And what about the nights when
we all climb into our grandparents' bed
and they move apart, making room for us
in the middle.

And maybe that's when my sister reads the part
I don't hear:
a baby coming. Another one. A brother or sister.
Still in her belly but coming soon.

She's coming to get us, my sister says again,
looking around
our big yellow kitchen. Then running her hand
over the hardwood table
as though she's already gone
and trying to remember this.

one morning,
late winter

Then one morning my grandfather is too sick
to walk the half mile to the bus
that takes him to work.

He stays in bed for the whole day
waking only to cough
and cough
and cough.

I walk slow around him
fluffing his pillows,
pressing cool cloths over his forehead
telling him the stories that come to me
again and again.

This I can do—find him another place to be
when this world is choking him.

Tell me a story, he says.

And I do.

new york baby

When my mother returns,
I will no longer be her baby girl.
I am sitting on my grandmother's lap
when she tells me this,
already so tall my legs dangle far down, the tips
of my toes touching the porch mat. My head
rests on her shoulder now where once,
it came only to her collarbone. She smells the way
she always does, of Pine-Sol and cotton,
Dixie Peach hair grease and something
warm and powdery.

I want to know whose baby girl I'll be
when my mother's new baby comes, born where
the sidewalks sparkle and me just a regular girl.

I didn't know how much I loved
being everyone's baby girl
until now when my life as baby girl
is nearly over.

leaving greenville

My mother arrives in the middle of the night,
and sleepily, we pile into her arms and hold tight.

Her kiss on the top of my head reminds me
of all that I love.

Mostly her.

It is late winter but my grandmother keeps
the window in our room slightly open
so that the cold fresh air can move over us
as we sleep. Two thick quilts and the three of us
side by side by side.

This is all we know now—

Cold pine breezes, my grandmother's quilts,
the heat of the wood-burning stove, the sweet
slow voices of the people around us,
red dust wafting, then settling as though it's said
all that it needs to say.

My mother tucks us back into our bed whispering,
We have a home up North now.

I am too sleepy to tell her that Greenville is home.
That even in the wintertime, the crickets
sing us to sleep.

And tomorrow morning, you'll get to meet
your new baby brother.

But I am already mostly asleep again, two arms
wrapped tight
around my mama's hand.

roman

His name is as strange as he is, this new baby brother
so pale and quiet and wide-eyed. He sucks his fist,
taking in all of us without blinking.
Another boy, Hope says,
now it's even-steven around here.

But I don't like the new baby of the family.
I want to send it back to wherever
babies live before they get here. When I pinch him,
a red mark stays behind, and his cry is high and tinny
a sound that hurts my ears.
That's what you get, my sister says.
His crying is him fighting you back.
Then she picks him up, holds him close,
tells him softly everything's all right,
everything's always going to be all right
until Roman gets quiet,
his wide black eyes looking only at Dell
as if
he believes her.

followed
the
sky's
mirrored
constellation
to
freedom

new york city

Maybe it's another New York City
the southerners talk about. Maybe that's where
there is money falling from the sky,
diamonds speckling
the sidewalks.

Here there is only gray rock, cold
and treeless as a bad dream. Who could love
this place—where no pine trees grow,
no porch swing moves
with the weight of
your grandmother.

This place is a Greyhound bus
humming through the night then letting out
a deep breath inside a place
called Port Authority. This place is a driver yelling,
New York City, last stop.
Everybody off.

This place is loud and strange
and nowhere I'm ever going to call
home.

brooklyn, new york

We did not stay in the small apartment
my mother found on Bristol Street,
Brownsville, Brooklyn, USA.

We did not stay because the dim bulb that hung
from a chain swung back and forth
when our upstairs neighbors walked
across their floor, casting shadows
that made my brother cry
and suck hard on his middle fingers.

We did not stay because the building was big and old
and when the bathroom ceiling fell
into the bathtub, my mother said,
I am not Henny Penny and that is not the sky!

So she called Aunt Kay and her boyfriend, Bernie,
they borrowed a truck and helped us pack,
bundled us up in winter coats
turned off that swinging light

and got us out of there!

herzl street

So we moved to Herzl Street
where Aunt Kay and Bernie lived upstairs.
And Peaches from Greenville lived below us.

And on Saturday nights more people
from Greenville came by
sitting and running their mouths
while the pots on the stove bubbled
with collards and sizzled with chicken
and corn bread baked up brown
inside Kay's big black oven.

And the people from Greenville
brought people from Spartanburg
and Charleston
and all of them talked
like our grandparents talked
and ate what we ate

so they were red dirt and pine trees
they were fireflies in jelly jars
and lemon-chiffon ice cream cones.

They were laughter on hot city nights
hot milk on cold city mornings,
good food and good times
fancy dancing and soul music.

They were family.

the johnny pump

Some days we miss
the way the red dirt lifted up and landed
against our bare feet. Here
the sidewalks burn hot all summer long.
Here we wear shoes. Broken bottles
don't always get swept up right away.

But our block has three johnny pumps
and a guy with a wrench
to turn them on. On the days when the heat
stops your breath, he comes up the block
pulling it out of his pocket. Then the johnny pump
is blasting cool water everywhere
and us and other kids running through it,
refreshed and laughing.

Even the grown-ups come out sometimes.
Once, I saw my
never-ever-barefoot-outside-in-the-city mother
take off her sandals,
stand at the curb
and let the cool water run over her feet.
She was looking up at the tiny piece of sky.
And she was smiling.

genetics

My mother has a gap between
her two front teeth. So does Daddy Gunnar.
Each child in this family has the same space
connecting us.

Our baby brother, Roman, was born pale as dust.
His soft brown curls and eyelashes stop
people on the street.
Whose angel child is this? they want to know.
When I say, *My brother,* the people
wear doubt
thick as a cape
until we smile
and the cape falls.

caroline but
we called her aunt kay,
some memories

Aunt Kay at the top of the stairs, her arms open,
her smile wide
and us running to her.

Aunt Kay dressed up on a Friday night
smelling of perfume,
her boyfriend, Bernie, her friend Peaches.

Aunt Kay in the kitchen with Peaches and Bernie
passing a blue-and-white box of Argo starch
back and forth, the hard white chunks of it,
disappearing into their mouths like candy,
the slow chew and swallow.

Aunt Kay and Mama and Peaches, in tight skirts
singing in a band.

Aunt Kay braiding my hair.

Aunt Kay running up the stairs to her own apartment
and me running behind her.

Aunt Kay laughing.

Aunt Kay hugging me.

Then a fall.
A crowd.
An ambulance.
My mother's tears.
A funeral.

And here, my Aunt Kay memories end.

moving again

After the falling
the stairs were all wrong to us.
Some days I head up there, my mother said,
forgetting that Kay is gone.

After the falling
Bernie and Peaches
packed their bags, moved out
to Far Rockaway, telling my mother
how much Kay loved the ocean.

After the falling
we took the A train
to their new apartment, played on the beach
till the sun went down, Mama quiet on a blanket
looking out at the water.

Kay was her big sister, only ten months older.
Everyone always thought they were twins
so that's what they said they were.

Couldn't look at one of us, my mother said,
without seeing the other.

After the falling
the hallway smelled
like Kay's perfume
whenever it rained

so we moved again
to the second floor of a pink house
on Madison Street.
Out front there was a five-foot sculpture
made from gray rock,
ivory and sand. A small fountain sent water
cascading over statues
of Mary, Joseph and Jesus.
People stopped in front of the house,
crossed themselves, mouthed a silent prayer
then moved on.

This house is protected, the landlord told my mother.
The saints keep us safe.
This house is protected, my mother whispered to us.
By the Saint of Ugly Sculpture.

After the falling
sometimes I would see my mother

smiling at that sculpture. And in her smile, there was Aunt Kay's smile, the two of them having a secret sister laugh, the two of them together again.

composition notebook

And somehow, one day, it's just there
speckled black-and-white, the paper
inside smelling like something I could fall right into,
live there—inside those clean white pages.

I don't know how my first composition notebook
ended up in my hands, long before I could really write
someone must have known that this
was all I needed.

Hard not to smile as I held it, felt the breeze
as I fanned the pages.
My sister thought my standing there
smiling was crazy
didn't understand how the smell and feel and sight
of bright white paper
could bring me so much joy.

And why does she need a notebook? She can't even write!

For days and days, I could only sniff the pages,
hold the notebook close
listen to the sound the papers made.

Nothing in the world is like this—
a bright white page with
pale blue lines. The smell of a newly sharpened pencil
the soft hush of it
moving finally
one day
into letters.

And even though she's smarter than anything,
this is something
my sister can't even begin
to understand.

on paper

The first time I write my full name

Jacqueline Amanda Woodson

without anybody's help
on a clean white page in my composition notebook,
  I know

if I wanted to

I could write anything.

Letters becoming words, words gathering meaning,
  becoming
thoughts outside my head

becoming sentences

written by

                              Jacqueline Amanda Woodson

saturday morning

Some days in this new place
there is only a box of pancake mix
an egg, and faucet water, the hiss
of those together
against a black cast-iron pan,
the pancakes sticking to it
syrupless but edible and us
complaining about it wishing like anything
we were back in Greenville,
where there was always something good
to eat. We remember
the collards growing
down south, the melons, fresh picked
and dripping with a sweetness New York
can never know.
We eat without complaining
or whining or asking our mother when there will be
syrup, butter, milk . . .
We remember Greenville
without her, count our blessings in silence
and chew.

first grade

My hand inside my sister's hand,
we walk the two blocks to P.S. 106—
I am six years old and
my sister tells me our school was once a castle.
I believe her. The school stretches for a full city block.
Inside
marble stairs wind their way to classrooms filled
with dark wood desks
nailed down to dark wood floors polished to a high
and beautiful shine.

I am in love with everything around me,
the dotted white lines moving
across my teacher's blackboard, the smell of chalk,
the flag jutting out from the wall and slowly swaying
above me.

There is nothing more beautiful than P.S. 106.
Nothing more perfect than my first-grade classroom.
No one more kind than Ms. Feidler, who meets me
at the door each morning,

takes my hand from my sister's, smiles down and says,
Now that Jacqueline is here, the day can finally begin.

And I believe her.
Yes, I truly believe her.

another kingdom hall

Because my grandmother calls and asks
if we're spreading Jehovah's word,
because my mother promises my grandmother
she'll raise us right in the eyes of God,
she finds a Kingdom Hall on Bushwick Avenue
so we can keep our Jehovah's Witness ways.
Every Sunday, we put on our Kingdom Hall clothes
pull out our Kingdom Hall satchels,
filled with our Kingdom Hall books
and walk the seven blocks
to the Kingdom Hall.

This is what reminds us of Greenville,
the Saturday-night pressing of satin ribbons,
Hope struggling with the knot in his tie,
our hair oiled and pulled back into braids,
our mother's hands less sure
than our grandmother's, the parts crooked, the braids
coming undone. And now, Dell and I
are left to iron our own dresses.
My hands,
my mother says,

as she stands at the sink, holding a crying Roman
with one hand,
her other holding a bottle of milk
under hot running water,
are full.

My mother drops us off at the Kingdom Hall door,
watches us walk
down the aisle to where Brothers and Sisters
are waiting
to help us turn the pages of our Bibles,
lean over to share their songbooks with us,
press Life Savers into our waiting hands . . .

Then our mother is gone, back home
or to a park bench,
where she'll sit and read until the meeting is over.
She has a full-time job now. Sunday, she says,
is her day of rest.

flag

When the kids in my class ask why
I am not allowed to pledge to the flag
I tell them *It's against my religion* but don't say,
I am in the world but not of the world. This,
they would not understand.
Even though my mother's not a Jehovah's Witness,
she makes us follow their rules and
leave the classroom when the pledge is being said.

Every morning, I walk out with Gina and Alina
the two other Witnesses in my class.
Sometimes, Gina says,
Maybe we should pray for the kids inside
who don't know that God said
"No other idols before me." That our God
is a jealous God.
Gina is the true believer. Her Bible open
during reading time. But Alina and I walk through
our roles as Witnesses as though this is the part
we've been given in a play
and once offstage, we run free, sing
"America the Beautiful" and "The Star-Spangled Banner"
far away from our families—knowing every word.

Alina and I want
more than anything to walk back into our classroom
press our hands against our hearts. Say,
"I pledge allegiance . . ." loud
without our jealous God looking down on us.
    Without our parents finding out.
Without our mothers' voices
in our heads saying, *You are different.*
Chosen.
Good.

When the pledge is over, we walk single file
back into the classroom, take our separate seats
Alina and I far away from Gina. But Gina
always looks back at us—as if to say,
I'm watching you. As if to say,
I know.

because we're witnesses

No Halloween.
No Christmas.
No birthdays.
Even when
other kids laugh as we leave the classroom
just as the birthday cupcakes arrive
we pretend we do not see the chocolate frosting,
pretend we do not want
to press our fingertips against
each colorful sprinkle and lift them,
one by sweet one
to our mouths.

No voting.
No fighting.
No cursing.
No wars.

We will never go to war.

We will never taste the sweetness of a classroom
birthday cupcake
We will never taste the bitterness of a battle.

brooklyn rain

The rain here is different than the way
it rains in Greenville. No sweet smell of honeysuckle.
No soft squish of pine. No slip and slide through grass.
Just Mama saying, *Stay inside today. It's raining,*
and me at the window. Nothing to do but
watch
the gray sidewalk grow darker,
watch
the drops slide down the glass pane,
watch
people below me move fast, heads bent.

Already there are stories
in my head. Already color and sound and words.
Already I'm
drawing circles on the glass, humming
myself someplace far away from here.

Down south, there was always someplace else to go
you could step out into the rain and
Grandma would let you
lift your head and stick out your tongue
be happy.

Down south already feels like a long time ago
but the stories in my head
take me back there, set me down in Daddy's garden
where the sun is always shining.

another way

While our friends are watching TV or playing outside,
we are in our house, knowing that begging our mother
to turn the television on is useless, begging her for
ten minutes outside will only mean her saying,
No. Saying,
You can run wild with your friends anytime. Today
I want you to find another way to play.

And then one day my mother
comes home with two shopping bags
filled with board games—Monopoly, checkers, chess,
Ants in the Pants, Sorry, Trouble,
just about every game we've ever seen
in the commercials between
our Saturday morning cartoons.

So many games, we don't know
where to begin playing, so we let Roman choose.
And he chooses Trouble
because he likes the sound the die makes
when it pops inside

its plastic bubble. And for days and days,
it is Christmas in November,
games to play when our homework is done,
Monopoly money to count
and checkers to slam down on boards, ants to flip
into blue plastic pants,
chess pieces to practice moving until we understand
their power
and when we don't, Roman and I argue
that there's another way to play
called *Our Way*. But Hope and Dell tell us
that we're too immature to even begin to understand
then bend over the chessboard in silence, each becoming
the next chess champ of the house, depending on the day
and the way the game is played.

Sometimes, Roman and I leave Hope and Dell alone
go to another corner of the room and become
what the others call us—*the two youngest*,
playing games we know the rules to
tic-tac-toe and checkers,
hangman and connect the dots

but mostly, we lean over their shoulders
as quietly as we can, watching
waiting
wanting to understand
how to play another way.

gifted

Everyone knows my sister
is brilliant. The letters come home folded neatly
inside official-looking envelopes that my sister proudly
hands over to my mother.
Odella has achieved
Odella has excelled at
Odella has been recommended to
Odella's outstanding performance in

She is gifted
we are told.
And I imagine presents surrounding her.

I am not gifted. When I read, the words twist
twirl across the page.
When they settle, it is too late.
The class has already moved on.

I want to catch words one day. I want to hold them
then blow gently,
watch them float
right out of my hands.

sometimes

There is only one other house on our block
where a father doesn't live. When somebody asks why,
the boy says, *He died.*
The girl looks off, down the block, her thumb
slowly rising to her mouth. The boy says,
I was a baby. Says, *She doesn't remember him*
and points to his silent sister.

Sometimes, I lie about my father.
He died, I say, *in a car wreck* or
He fell off a roof or maybe
He's coming soon.
Next week and
next week and
next week . . . but
if my sister's nearby
she shakes her head. Says,
She's making up stories again.
Says,
We don't have a father anymore.
Says,
Our grandfather's our father now.
Says,
Sometimes, that's the way things happen.

uncle robert

Uncle Robert has moved to New York City!

I hear him taking the stairs
two at a time and then
he is at our door, knocking loud until our mother
   opens it,
curlers in her hair, robe pulled closed, whispering,
It's almost midnight, don't you wake my children!

But we are already awake, all four of us, smiling
   and jumping around
my uncle: *What'd you bring me?*

Our mama shushes us, says,
It's too late for presents and the like.
But we want presents and the like.
And she, too, is smiling now, happy to see her
   baby brother who lives all the way over
in Far Rockaway where the ocean is right there
if you look out your window.

Robert opens his hand to reveal a pair of silver earrings,
says to my sister, *This is a gift for how smart you are.*
I want

to be smart like Dell, I want
someone to hand me silver and gold
just because my brain clicks into thinking whenever
it needs to but
I am not smart like Dell so I watch her press
    the silver moons into her ears
I say, *I know a girl ten times smarter than her. She gets*
    diamonds every time she gets a hundred on a test.
    And Robert looks at me, his dark eyes smiling, asks,
    Is that something you made up? Or something real?
In my own head,
it's real as anything.

In my head
all kinds of people are doing all kinds of things.
I want to tell him this, that
the world we're living in right here in Bushwick isn't
the only place. But now my brothers are asking,

What'd you bring me, and my uncle is pulling gifts
    from his pockets,
from his leather briefcase, from inside his socks.
    He hands
my mother a record, a small 45—James Brown,
    who none of us
like because he screams when he sings. But my mother
    puts it on the record player, turned way down low
    and then even us kids are dancing around—

Robert showing us the steps he learned
at the Far Rockaway parties. His feet are magic
and we all try to slide across the floor like he does,
our own feet, again and again,
betraying us.

Teach us, Robert! we keep saying. *Teach us!*

wishes

When he takes us to the park, Uncle Robert tells us,
If you catch a dandelion puff, you can make a wish.
Anything you want will come true, he says as
we chase the feathery wishes around swings,
beneath sliding boards,
until we can hold them in our hands,
close our eyes tight, whisper our dream
then set it floating out into the universe hoping
our uncle is telling the truth,
hoping each thing we wish for
will one day come true.

believing

The stories start like this—

Jack and Jill went up a hill, my uncle sings.
I went up a hill yesterday, I say.
What hill?
In the park.
What park?
Halsey Park.
Who was with you?
Nobody.
But you're not allowed to go to the park without anyone.
I just did.
Maybe you dreamed it, my uncle says.
No, I really went.

And my uncle likes the stories I'm making up.

. . . Along came a spider and sat down beside her.
I got bit by a spider, I say.
When?
The other day.
Where?

Right on my foot.
Show us.
It's gone now.

But my mother accuses me of lying.
If you lie, she says, *one day you'll steal.*

I won't steal.
It's hard to understand how one leads to the other,
how stories could ever
make us criminals.

It's hard to understand
the way my brain works—so different
from everybody around me.
How each new story
I'm told becomes a thing
that happens,
in some other way
to me . . . !

Keep making up stories, my uncle says.
You're lying, my mother says.

Maybe the truth is somewhere in between
all that I'm told
and memory.

off-key

We start each meeting at Kingdom Hall with a song
and a prayer
but we're always late,
walking in when the pink songbooks are already open,
looking over shoulders, asking Brothers and Sisters
to help us find our place.
If it's a song I like, I sing loud until my sister shushes me
with a finger to her mouth.

My whole family knows I can't sing. My voice,
my sister says, is just left of the key. Just right
of the tune.

But I sing anyway, whenever I can.

Even the boring Witness songs sound good to me,
    the words
telling us how God wants us to behave,
what he wants us to do,
Be glad you nations with his people! Go preach
    from door to door!

The good news of Jehovah's kingdom—
Proclaim from shore to shore!

It's the music around the words that I hear
in my head, even though
everyone swears I *can't* hear it.
Strange that they don't hear
what I hear.

Strange that it sounds so right

to me.

eve and the snake

The Sunday sermons are given by men.
Women aren't allowed to get onstage like this,
standing alone to tell God's story. I don't
understand why but I listen anyway:

On the first day, God made the heavens and the earth
and He looked at it, and it was good.

It's a long story. It's a good story.
Adam and Eve got made,
a snake appeared in a tree. A talking snake.
Then Eve had to make a choice—the apple the snake
    wanted her to eat
looked so good—just one bite. But it was the only apple
    in a kingdom full of apples
that God had said *Don't touch!*

It's the best apple in all the world, the snake said.
    Go ahead and taste it. God won't care.

But we know the ending—in our heads, we scream,
Don't do it, Eve! That's the Devil inside that snake!
    He's tricking you!

But Eve took a bite. And so here we are,
sitting in a Kingdom Hall
on a beautiful Sunday afternoon
hoping that God sees it in His heart to know
it wasn't our fault. Give us another chance
send that snake back and we promise
we'll say no this time!

our father, fading away

In all our moving, we've forgotten our family in Ohio,
forgotten our father's voice, the slow drawl
of his words,
the way he and his brother David made jokes
that weren't funny
and laughed as though they were.

We forget the color of his skin—was it
dark brown like mine or lighter like Dell's?
Did he have Hope and Dell's loose curls or my
tighter, kinkier hair?

Was his voice deep or high?
Was he a hugger like Grandma Georgiana holding us
like she never planned to let go or
did he hug hard and fast like Mama,
planting her warm lips to our foreheads where
the kiss lingered
long after
she said I love you, pulled her sweater on and left
for work each morning.

In Brooklyn there are no more calls from Ohio.
No more calls from our father or Grandpa Hope
or Grandma Grace
or David or Anne or Ada or Alicia.

It is as if each family
has disappeared from the other.

Soon, someone who knows someone in Ohio
    who knows the Woodsons
tells my mother that Grandpa Hope has died.
At dinner that evening, our mother gives us the news but
we keep eating because we hadn't known
he was still alive.

And for a moment, I think about Jack . . . our father.
But then
quickly as it comes
the thought moves on.

Out of sight, out of mind, my brother says.

But only a part of me believes this is true.

halfway home #2

For a long time, there is only one tree on our block.
And though it still feels
strange to be so far away from soft dirt
beneath bare feet
the ground is firm here and the one tree blooms
wide enough to shade four buildings.
The city is settling around me, my words
   come fast now
when I speak, the soft curl of the South on my tongue
is near gone.

Who are these city children? My grandmother laughs,
   her own voice
sad and far away on the phone. But it is
   a long-distance call
from Greenville to Brooklyn, too much money
and not enough time to explain
that New York City is gray rock
and quick-moving cars.
That the traffic lights change fast and my sister must
hold tight to my hand
as we cross to where a small man singing

Piragua! Piragua!
sells shaved ices from a white cart filled
with bottles and bottles of fruit-flavored syrup
colored red and purple, orange and blue.
That our mouths water in the hot sun as we hand him
our quarters then wait patiently as he pours
    the syrup over the ice, hands it to us
in paper cones.

We'll be coming home soon, Grandma
each of us promises.
We love you.

And when she says, *I love you, too*
the South is so heavy in her mouth
my eyes fill up with the missing of
everything and everyone
I've ever known.

the paint eater

In the night in the corner of the bedroom
the four of us share,
comes a pick, pick, picking of plaster
paint gone come morning.

My younger brother, Roman,
can't explain why paint melting
on his tongue feels good.

Still, he eats the paint
and plaster until a white hole
grows where pale green paint used to be.

And too late we catch him,
his fingers in his mouth,
his lips covered with dust.

chemistry

When Hope speaks, it's always about comic books
and superheroes
until my mother tells him he has to talk
about something else.
And then it's science. He wants to know
everything
about rockets and medicine and the galaxy.
He wants to know where the sky ends and how,
what does it feel like when gravity's gone
and what is the food men eat
on the moon. His questions come so fast
and so often that we forget how quiet
he once was until my mother
buys him a chemistry set.

And then for hours after school each day
he makes potions, mixing chemicals that stink up
the house, causing sparks to fly
from shaved bits of iron,
puffs of smoke to pop from strange-colored liquids.
We are fascinated by him, goggled and bent
over the stove

a clamped test tube protruding
from his gloved hand.

On the days when our mother says
she doesn't want him smelling up the house
with his potions, he takes his trains apart, studies
each tiny piece, then slowly puts them together again.

We don't know what it is he's looking for
as he searches the insides of things, studies
the way things change. Each whispered *Wow*
from him makes me think that he
with his searching—and Dell with her reading
and even Roman with his trying to eat
to the other side of our walls—is looking
for something. Something way past Brooklyn.
Something
out
there.

baby in the house

And then one day, Roman won't get up,
sun coming in bright
through the bedroom window, the rest of us
dressed and ready to go outside.
No laughter—just tears when we hold him.
More crying when we put him down.
Won't eat and even my mother
can't help him.

When she takes him to the hospital, she comes back

alone.

And for many days after that, there is no baby
in our house and I am finally
the baby girl again, wishing

I wasn't. Wishing there wasn't so much quiet
where my brother's laugh used to be, wishing

the true baby in our house
was home.

going home again

July comes and Robert takes us on the night train
back to South Carolina. We kiss
our baby brother good-bye in his hospital bed where
he reaches out, cries to come with us.

His words are weak as water, no more
than a whisper with so much air around them.

I'm coming too, he says.

But he isn't coming.
Not this time.
My mother says there is lead in his blood
from the paint he finds a way to pick
and eat off our bedroom wall
every time our backs are turned.
Small holes grow, like white stars against
the green paint, covered again and again
by our mother. But still, he finds a way.

Each of us hugs him, promises
to bring him candy and toys.

Promises we won't have fun down south
without him.

Each of us leans in
for our mother's kiss on our forehead,
her warm lips, already a memory

that each of us carries home.

home again to hall street

My grandmother's kitchen is the same
big and yellow and smelling of the pound cake
she's made to welcome us back.

And now in the late afternoon, she is standing
at the sink, tearing collards beneath
cool running water, while the crows caw outside,
and the sun sinks slow into red and gold

When Hope lets the screen door slam,
she fusses,
Boy, don't you slam my door again! and my brother says,
I'm sorry.

Just like always.

Soon, there'll be lemonade on the porch,
the swing whining the same early evening song
it always sings
my brother and sister with the checker set between them
me next to my grandfather, falling asleep against
his thin shoulder.

And it's not even strange that it feels the way
    it's always felt
like the place we belong to.

Like *home*.

mrs. hughes's house

In Greenville, my grandfather is too sick
to work anymore, so my grandmother has a full-time job.
Now we spend every day from July
until the middle of August
at Mrs. Hughes's Nursery and Day School.

Each morning, we walk the long dusty road
to Mrs. Hughes's house—large, white stone,
with a yard circling and chickens pecking at our feet.
Beyond the yard there's collards and corn growing
a scarecrow, black snakes, and whip-poor-wills.

She is a big woman, tall, yellow-skinned and thick
    as a wall.
I hold tight to my grandmother's hand. Maybe
    I am crying.

My grandmother drops us off and
the other kids circle around us. Laughing at
our hair, our clothes, the names our parents
have given us,

our city way of talking—too fast, too many words
to hear at once
too many big words coming out of
my sister's mouth.

I am always the first to cry. A gentle slap on the side
of my head, a secret pinch,
girls circling around me singing, *Who stole the cookie
from the cookie jar* and
pointing, as though the song is true, at me.

My sister's tears are slow to come. But when they do,
it isn't sadness.
It's something different that sends her swinging
    her fists when
the others yank her braids until the satin,
newly ironed ribbons belong to them,
hidden away in the deep pockets of their dresses,
tucked into
their sagging stockings, buried inside their
silver lunch pails.

Hope is silent—his name, they say, belongs to a girl,
his ears, they laugh
stick out too far from his head.

Our feet are beginning to belong
in two different worlds—Greenville

and New York. We don't know how to come
home
and leave
home
behind us.

how to listen #4

Kids are mean, Dell says.
Just turn away. Pretend we
know better than that.

field service

Saturday morning's the hardest day for us now.
For three hours we move through
the streets of Nicholtown,
knocking on strangers' doors, hoping to convert
them into Sisters and Brothers and children of God.

This summer I am allowed to knock on my first door
alone. An old woman answers, smiles kindly at me.
What a special child you are, she says.
Sky-blue ribbons in my hair, my *Watchtower* held tight
in my white-gloved hand,
the blue linen dress a friend of my grandmother's
has made for me stopping just above my knees.

My name is Jacqueline Woodson, I nearly whisper,
my throat suddenly dry
voice near gone.
I'm here to bring you some good news today . . .

Well how much does your good news cost, the woman
    wants to know.

A dime.

She shakes her head sadly, closes her door a moment
to search beneath a trunk where she hopes
she's dropped a coin or two.
But when she comes back, there are no coins
in her hand.
Oh I'd love to read that magazine, she says.
I just don't have money.

And for many days my heart hurts with the sadness
that such a nice woman will not be a part of God's
    new world.
It isn't fair, I say to my grandmother when
so many days have passed.
I want to go back. I want to give her something
    for free.

But we're done now with that strip of Nicholtown.
Next Saturday, we'll be somewhere else.
Another Witness will go there, my grandmother promises.
By and by, she says, *that woman will find her way.*

sunday afternoon
on the front porch

Across the road,
Miss Bell has tied a blue-checked sunbonnet
beneath her chin, lifts her head from her bed
of azaleas and waves to my grandmother.
I am sitting beside her on the front porch swing, Hope
and Dell leaning back against the wood beam
at the top of the front porch stairs. It is as
though we have always been in this position,
the front porch swing moving gently back and forth,
the sun warm on our faces, the day only halfway over.

I see your grands are back for the summer,
   Miss Bell says. *Getting big, too.*

It is Sunday afternoon.
Out back, my grandfather pulls weeds from his garden,
digs softly into the rich earth to add new melon seeds.
   Wondering
if this time, they'll grow. All this he does from
a small chair, a cane beside him.
He moves as if underwater, coughs

hard and long into a handkerchief, calls out for Hope
when he needs the chair moved, sees me watching,
and shakes his head. *I'm catching you worrying,* he says.
Too young for that. So just cut it out now, you hear?
His voice
so strong and clear today, I can't help smiling.

Soon I'll rise from the porch,
change out of my Kingdom Hall clothes into
a pair of shorts and a cotton blouse
trade my patent-leather Mary Janes for bare feet
and join my grandfather in the garden.

What took you so long, he'll say. *I was about to turn
this earth around without you.*

Soon, it'll be near evening and Daddy and I
will walk slow
back into the house where I'll pull the Epsom salt
from the shelf
fill the dishpan with warm water, massage
his swelling hands.

But for now, I sit listening to Nicholtown settle
around me,
pray that one day Roman will be well enough
to know this moment.

Pray that we will always have this—the front porch,
my grandfather in the garden,
a woman in a blue-checked sunbonnet
moving through azaleas . . .

Pretty children, Miss Bell says.
But God don't make them no other kinda way.

home then home again

Too fast, our summer in Greenville
is ending.
Already, the phone calls from my mother
are filled with plans for coming home.
We miss
our little's brother's laughter, the way
he runs to us at the end of the school day as if
we've been gone forever. The way his small hands
curl around ours when we watch TV. Holding
tight through the scary parts, until we tell him
Scooby-Doo will save the day,
Bugs Bunny will get away,
Underdog will arrive before the train hits
Sweet Polly Purebred.

We drag our feet below our swings,
our arms wrapped lazily around the metal links
no longer fascinated by the newness
of the set, the way we climbed all over the slide,
pumped our legs hard—toward heaven until
the swing set shook with the weight of us lifting it
from the ground.

Next summer, my grandfather said, *I'll cement it down.*
But in the meantime
you all swing low.

Our suitcases sit at the foot of our bed, open
slowly filling with freshly washed summer clothes,
each blouse, each pair of shorts, each faded cotton dress
holding a story that we'll tell again and again
all winter long.

deep
in
my heart,
i do
believe

family

In the books, there's always a happily ever after.
The ugly duckling grows into a swan, Pinocchio
becomes a boy.
The witch gets chucked into the oven by Gretel,
the Selfish Giant goes to heaven.
Even Winnie the Pooh seems to always get his honey.
Little Red Riding Hood's grandmother is freed
from the belly of the wolf.

When my sister reads to me, I wait for the moment
when the story moves faster—toward the happy ending
that I know is coming.

On the bus home from Greenville, I wake to the almost
happy ending, my mother standing at the station, Roman
in his stroller, his smile bright, his arms reaching for us
but we see the white hospital band like a bracelet
on his wrist. Tomorrow he will return there.

We are not all finally and safely
home.

one place

For a long time, our little brother
goes back and forth to the hospital, his body
weak from the lead, his brain
not doing what a brain is supposed to do. We don't
understand why he's so small, has tubes
coming from his arms, sleeps and sleeps . . .
when we visit him.

But one day,
he comes home. The holes in the wall
are covered over and left
unpainted, his bed pulled away from *temptation,*
nothing for him to peel away.

He is four now, curls long gone, his dark brown hair
straight as a bone, strange to us but
our little brother, the four of us again

in one place.

maria

Late August now
home from Greenville and ready
for what the last of the summer brings me.
All the dreams this city holds
right outside—just step through the door and walk
two doors down to where
my new best friend, Maria, lives. Every morning,
I call up to her window, *Come outside*
or she rings our bell, *Come outside.*
Her hair is crazily curling down past her back,
the Spanish she speaks like a song
I am learning to sing.
Mi amiga, Maria.
Maria, my friend.

how to listen #5

What is your one dream,
my friend Maria asks me.
Your one wish come true?

tomboy

My sister, Dell, reads and reads
and never learns
to jump rope or
play handball against the factory wall on the corner.
Never learns to sprint
barefoot down the block
to become
the fastest girl
on Madison Street.
Doesn't learn
to hide the belt or steal the bacon
or kick the can . . .
But I do and because of this
Tomboy becomes my new name.
My walk, my mother says,
reminds her of my father.
When I move long-legged and fast away from her
she remembers him.

game over

When my mother calls,
Hope Dell Jackie—inside!
the game is over.
No more reading beneath the streetlight
for Dell. But for my brother and me
it's no more *anything!* No more
steal the bacon
coco levio 1-2-3
Miss Lucy had a baby
spinning tops
double Dutch.
No more
freeze tag
hide the belt
hot peas and butter.
No more
singing contests on the stoop.
No more
ice cream truck chasing:
Wait! Wait, ice cream man! My mother's gonna
give me money!
No more getting wet in the johnny pump

or standing with two fisted hands out in front of me,
a dime hidden in one, chanting,
Dumb school, dumb school, which hand's it in?

When my mother calls,
Hope Dell Jackie—inside!
we complain as we walk up the block in the twilight:
Everyone else is allowed to stay outside till dark.
Our friends standing in the moment—
string halfway wrapped around a top,
waiting to be tagged and unfrozen,
searching for words to a song,
dripping from the johnny pump,
silent in the middle of *Miss Lucy had a . . .*

The game is over for the evening and all we can hear
is our friends'
Aw . . . man!!
Bummer!
For real?! This early?!
Dang it!
Shoot. Your mama's mean!
Early birds!
Why she gotta mess up our playing like that?
Jeez. Now
the game's over!

lessons

My mother says:

When Mama tried to teach me

to make collards and potato salad
I didn't want to learn.

She opens the box of pancake mix, adds milk
and egg, stirs. I watch
grateful for the food we have now—syrup waiting
in the cabinet, bananas to slice on top.
It's Saturday morning.
Five days a week, she leaves us
to work at an office back in Brownsville.
Saturday we have her to ourselves, all day long.

Me and Kay didn't want to be inside cooking.

She stirs the lumps from the batter, pours it
into the buttered, hissing pan.

Wanted to be with our friends
running wild through Greenville.

There was a man with a peach tree down the road.
One day Robert climbed over that fence, filled a bucket
with peaches. Wouldn't share them with any of us but
told us where the peach tree was. And that's where we
wanted to be
sneaking peaches from that man's tree, throwing
the rotten ones
at your uncle!

Mama wanted us to learn to cook.

Ask the boys, we said. And Mama knew that wasn't fair
girls inside and boys going off to steal peaches!
So she let all of us
stay outside until suppertime.

And by then, she says, putting our breakfast on the table,

it was too late.

trading places

When Maria's mother makes
arroz con habichuelas y tostones,
we trade dinners. If it's a school night,
I'll run to Maria's house, a plate of my mother's
baked chicken with Kraft mac and cheese,
sometimes box corn bread,
sometimes canned string beans,
warm in my hands, ready for the first taste
of Maria's mother's garlicky rice and beans,
crushed green bananas
fried and salted and warm . . .

Maria will be waiting, her own plate covered in foil.
   Sometimes
we sit side by side on her stoop, our traded plates
in our laps.
What are you guys eating? the neighborhood kids ask
but we never answer, too busy shoveling the food we love
into our mouths.
Your mother makes the best chicken, Maria says. *The best
corn bread. The best everything!*
Yeah, I say.
I guess my grandma taught her something after all.

writing #1

It's easier to make up stories
than it is to write them down. When I speak,
the words come pouring out of me. The story
wakes up and walks all over the room. Sits in a chair,
crosses one leg over the other, says,
Let me introduce myself. Then just starts going on and on.
But as I bend over my composition notebook,
only my name
comes quickly. Each letter, neatly printed
between the pale blue lines. Then white
space and air and me wondering, *How do I*
spell introduce? Trying again and again
until there is nothing but pink
bits of eraser and a hole now
where a story should be.

late autumn

Ms. Moskowitz calls us one by one and says,
Come up to the board and write your name.
When it's my turn, I walk down the aisle from
my seat in the back, write *Jacqueline Woodson—*
the way I've done a hundred times, turn back
toward my seat, proud as anything
of my name in white letters on the dusty blackboard.
But Ms. Moskowitz stops me, says,
In cursive too, please. But the *q* in Jacqueline is too hard
so I write *Jackie Woodson* for the first time. Struggle
only a little bit with the *k.*

Is that what you want us to call you?

I want to say, *No, my name is Jacqueline*
but I am scared of that cursive *q,* know
I may never be able to connect it to *c* and *u*
so I nod even though
I am lying.

the other woodson

Even though so many people think my sister and I
are twins,
I am the other Woodson, following behind her each year
into the same classroom she had the year before. Each
teacher smiles when they call my name. *Woodson,* they
say. *You must be Odella's sister.* Then they nod
slowly, over and over again, call me Odella. Say,
I'm sorry! You look so much like her and she is SO brilliant!
then wait for my brilliance to light up
the classroom. Wait for my arm to fly into
the air with every answer. Wait for my pencil
to move quickly through the too-easy math problems
on the mimeographed sheet. Wait for me to stand
before class, easily reading words even high school
students stumble over. And they keep waiting.
And waiting
and waiting
and waiting

until one day, they walk into the classroom,
almost call me Odel—then stop

remember that I am the other Woodson

and begin searching for brilliance

at another desk.

writing #2

On the radio, Sly and the Family Stone are singing
"Family Affair," the song turned up because it's
my mother's favorite, the one she plays again and again.

You can't leave 'cause your heart is there, Sly sings.
But you can't stay 'cause you been somewhere else.

The song makes me think of Greenville and Brooklyn
the two worlds my heart lives in now. I am writing
the lyrics down, trying to catch each word
   before it's gone

then reading them back, out loud to my mother. This
is how I'm learning. Words come slow to me
on the page until
I memorize them, reading the same books over
and over, copying
lyrics to songs from records and TV commercials,
the words
settling into my brain, into my memory.
Not everyone learns

to read this way—memory taking over when the rest
of the brain stops working,
but I do.

Sly is singing the words
over and over as though
he is trying
to convince me that this whole world
is just a bunch of families
like ours

going about their own family affairs.

Stop daydreaming, my mother says.

So I go back to writing down words
that are songs and stories and whole new worlds
tucking themselves into
my memory.

birch tree poem

Before my teacher reads the poem,
she has to explain.
A birch, she says, *is a kind of tree*
then magically she pulls a picture
from her desk drawer and the tree is suddenly
real to us.

"When I see birches bend to left and right . . ." she begins
"Across the lines of straighter darker trees,
I like to think"—

and when she reads, her voice drops down so low
and beautiful
some of us put our heads on our desks to keep
the happy tears from flowing

—*"some boy's been swinging them.*
But swinging doesn't bend them down to stay
As ice-storms do."

And even though we've never seen an ice storm
we've seen a birch tree, so we can imagine
everything we need to imagine

forever and ever

infinity

amen.

how to listen #6

When I sit beneath
the shade of my block's oak tree
the world disappears.

reading

I am not my sister.
Words from the books curl around each other
make little sense
until
I read them again
and again, the story
settling into memory. *Too slow*
the teacher says.
Read faster.
Too babyish, the teacher says.
Read older.
But I don't want to read faster or older or
any way else that might
make the story disappear too quickly from where
    it's settling
inside my brain,
slowly becoming
a part of me.
A story I will remember
long after I've read it for the second, third,
tenth, hundredth time.

stevie and me

Every Monday, my mother takes us
to the library around the corner. We are allowed
to take out seven books each. On those days,
no one complains
that all I want are picture books.

Those days, no one tells me to read faster
to read harder books
to read like Dell.

No one is there to say, *Not that book,*
when I stop in front of the small paperback
with a brown boy on the cover.
Stevie.

I read:
One day my momma told me,
"You know you're gonna have
a little friend come stay with you."
And I said, "Who is it?"

If someone had been fussing with me
to read like my sister, I might have missed

the picture book filled with brown people, more
brown people than I'd ever seen
in a book before.

The little boy's name was Steven but
his mother kept calling him Stevie.
My name is Robert but my momma don't
call me Robertie.

If someone had taken
that book out of my hand
said, *You're too old for this*
maybe
I'd never have believed
that someone who looked like me
could be in the pages of the book
that someone who looked like me
had a story.

when i tell my family

When I tell my family
I want to be a writer, they smile and say,
We see you in the backyard with your writing.
They say,
We hear you making up all those stories.
And,
We used to write poems.
And,
It's a good hobby, we see how quiet it keeps you.
They say,
But maybe you should be a teacher,
a lawyer,
do hair . . .

I'll think about it, I say.

And maybe all of us know

this is just another one of my
stories.

daddy gunnar

Saturday morning and Daddy Gunnar's voice
is on the other end of the phone.
We all grab for it.
Let me speak to him!
My turn!
No mine!
Until Mama makes us stand in line.

He coughs hard, takes deep breaths.
When he speaks, it's almost low as a whisper.

How are my New York grandbabies, he wants to know.

We're good, I say, holding tight to the phone
but my sister is already grabbing for it,
Hope and even Roman, all of us
hungry for the sound
of his faraway voice.

Y'all know how much I love you?

Infinity and back again, I say
the way I've said it a million times.

And then, Daddy says to me, *Go on and add
a little bit more to that.*

hope onstage

Until the curtain comes up and he's standing there,
ten years old and alone in the center of the P.S. 106 stage,
no one knew
my big brother could sing. He is dressed
   as a shepherd, his voice
soft and low, more sure than any sound I've ever heard
come out of him. My quiet big brother
   who only speaks
when asked, has little to say to any of us, except
when he's talking about science or comic books, now
has a voice that is circling the air,
landing clear and sweet around us:

"Tingalayo, come little donkey come.
Tingalayo, come little donkey come.
My donkey walks, my donkey talks
my donkey eats with a knife and fork.
Oh Tingalayo, come little donkey come."

Hope can sing . . . my sister says in wonder
   as my mother
and the rest of the audience start to clap.

Maybe, I am thinking, there is something hidden
like this, in all of us. A small gift from the universe
waiting to be discovered.

My big brother raises his arms, calling his donkey home.
He is smiling as he sings, the music getting louder
behind him.

"Tingalayo . . ."

And in the darkened auditorium, the light
is only on Hope
and it's hard to believe he has such a magic
    singing voice
and even harder to believe his donkey
is going to come running.

daddy this time

Greenville is different this summer,

Roman is well and out back, swinging hard. Somewhere
between last summer and now, our daddy
cemented the swing set down.
Roman doesn't know the shaky days—just this moment,
his dark blue Keds pointing toward the sky,
     his laughter and screams, like wind
through the screen door.
Now my grandmother shushes him,
Daddy resting in the bedroom, the covers pulled up
     to his chin,
his thin body so much smaller than I remember it.

Just a little tired, Daddy says to me, when I tiptoe
in with chicken soup,
sit on the edge of the bed and try to get him
to take small sips.
He struggles into sitting, lets me feed him
small mouthfuls but only a few
are enough. *Too tired to eat anymore.*
Then he closes his eyes.

Outside, Roman laughs again and the swing set
whines with the weight of him.
Maybe Hope is there, pushing him
into the air. Or maybe it's Dell.
The three of them would rather be outside.

His room smells, my sister says.
But I don't smell anything except the lotion
I rub into my grandfather's hands.
When the others aren't around, he whispers,
    You're my favorite,
smiles and winks at me. *You're going to be fine,*
    you know that.
Then he coughs hard and closes his eyes, his breath
struggling to get
into and out of his body.

Most days, I am in here with my grandfather,
    holding his hand
while he sleeps
fluffing pillows and telling him stories
about my friends back home.
When he asks, I speak to him in Spanish,
the language that rolls off my tongue
like I was born knowing it.
Sometimes, my grandfather says,
Sing me something pretty.

And when I sing to him, I'm not
just left of the key or right of the tune
He says I sing beautifully.

He says I am perfect.

what everybody
knows now

Even though the laws have changed
my grandmother still takes us
to the back of the bus when we go downtown
in the rain. *It's easier,* my grandmother says,
than having white folks look at me like I'm dirt.

But we aren't dirt. We are people
paying the same fare as other people.
When I say this to my grandmother,
she nods, says, *Easier to stay where you belong.*

I look around and see the ones
who walk straight to the back. See
the ones who take a seat up front, daring
anyone to make them move. And know
this is who I want to be. Not scared
like that. Brave
like that.

Still, my grandmother takes my hand downtown
pulls me right past the restaurants that have to let us sit

wherever we want now. *No need in making trouble,*
she says. *You all go back to New York City but*
I have to live here.

We walk straight past Woolworth's
without even looking in the windows
because the one time my grandmother went inside
they made her wait and wait. *Acted like*
I wasn't even there. It's hard *not* to see the moment—
my grandmother in her Sunday clothes, a hat
with a flower pinned to it
neatly on her head, her patent-leather purse,
perfectly clasped
between her gloved hands—waiting quietly
long past her turn.

end of summer

Too fast the summer leaves us, we kiss
our grandparents good-bye and my uncle Robert
is there waiting
to take us home again.

When we hug our grandfather, his body
is all bones and skin. But he is up now,
sitting at the window, a blanket covering
his thin shoulders.

Soon, I'll get back to that garden, he says.
But most days, all I want to do
is lay down and rest.

We wave again from the taxi that pulls out
slow down the drive—watch our grandmother,
still waving,
grow small behind us and our grandfather,
in the window,
fade from sight.

far rockaway

Robert only stays long enough
for my mother to thank him
for buying our tickets
for getting us home.

He does a fancy turn on his heel, aims
two pointer fingers at us
says, *I'll catch up with all of you later.*

We tell him that he has to come back soon,
remind him of all the stuff he's promised us
trips to Coney Island and Palisades Amusement Park,
    a Crissy doll
with hair that grows, a Tonka toy, *Gulliver's Travels*,
    candy.

He says he won't forget,
asks us if he's a man of his word and
everyone except my mother
nods.

Hard not to miss my mother's eyebrows,
giving her baby brother a look,

pressing her lips together. Once,
in the middle of the night, two policemen
knocked on our door, asking for Robert Leon Irby.
But my uncle wasn't here.

So now my mother takes a breath, says,
Stay safe.
Says,
Don't get into trouble out there, Robert.

He gives her a hug, promises he won't
and then he is gone.

fresh air

When I get back to Brooklyn, Maria isn't there.
She's gone upstate, staying with a family,
her mother tells me, that has a pool. Then her mother
puts a plate of food in front of me, tells me
how much she knows I love her rice and chicken.

When Maria returns she is tanned and wearing
a new short set. Everything about her seems different.
I stayed with white people, she tells me. *Rich white people.*
The air upstate is different. It doesn't smell like anything!
She hands me a piece of bubble gum with BUBBLE YUM
in bright letters.
This is what they chew up there.
The town was called Schenectady.

All the rest of the summer Maria and I buy only
   Bubble Yum, blow
huge bubbles while I make her tell me story after
story about the white family in Schenectady.

They kept saying I was poor and trying to give me stuff,
Maria says. *I had to keep telling them it's not poor*
where we live.

Next summer, I say. *You should just come down south.*
It's different there.

And Maria promises she will.

On the sidewalk we draw hopscotch games that we
play using chipped pieces of slate, chalk
Maria & Jackie Best Friends Forever wherever
there is smooth stone.
Write it so many times that it's hard to walk
on our side
of the street without looking down
and seeing us there.

p.s. 106 haiku

Jacqueline Woodson.
I'm finally in fourth grade.
It's raining outside.

learning from langston

I loved my friend.

He went away from me.
There's nothing more to say.
The poem ends,
Soft as it began—
I loved my friend.
   —Langston Hughes

   I love my friend
and still do
when we play games
we laugh. I hope she never goes away from me
   because I love my friend.
   —Jackie Woodson

the selfish giant

In the story of the Selfish Giant, a little boy hugs
a giant who has never been hugged before.
The giant falls
in love with the boy but then one day,
the boy disappears.
When he returns, he has scars on his hands and
his feet, just like Jesus.
The giant dies and goes to Paradise.

The first time my teacher reads the story to the class
I cry all afternoon, and am still crying
when my mother gets home from work that evening.

She doesn't understand why
I want to hear such a sad story again and again
but takes me to the library around the corner
when I beg
and helps me find the book to borrow.
The Selfish Giant, by Oscar Wilde.

I read the story again and again.

Like the giant, I, too, fall in love with the Jesus boy,
there's something so sweet about him, I want
to be his friend.

Then one day, my teacher asks me to come up front
to read out loud. But I don't need to bring
the book with me.
The story of the Selfish Giant is in my head now,
living there. Remembered.

"Every afternoon, as they were coming from school,
the children used to go and play in the Giant's garden . . ."
I tell the class, the whole story flowing out of me
right up to the end when the boy says,

"These are the wounds of Love . . .
"You let me play once in your garden, today you shall
come with me to my garden, which is Paradise . . ."

How did you do that, my classmates ask.
How did you memorize all those words?

But I just shrug, not knowing what to say.
How can I explain to anyone that stories
are like air to me,
I breathe them in and let them out
over and over again.

Brilliant! my teacher says, smiling.
Jackie, that was absolutely beautiful.

And I know now
words are my Tingalayo. Words are my brilliance.

the butterfly poems

No one believes me when I tell them
I am writing a book about butterflies,
even though they see me with the *Childcraft* encyclopedia
heavy on my lap opened to the pages where
the monarch, painted lady, giant swallowtail and
queen butterflies live. Even one called a buckeye.

When I write the first words
Wings of a butterfly whisper . . .

no one believes a whole book could ever come
from something as simple as
butterflies that *don't even,* my brother says,
live that long.

But on paper, things can live forever.
On paper, a butterfly
never dies.

six minutes

The Sisters in the Kingdom Hall get six minutes
to be onstage. In pairs. Or threes.
But never alone.
We have to write skits
where we are visiting another Sister
or maybe a nonbeliever. Sometimes
the play takes place at their pretend kitchen table
and sometimes, we're in their pretend living room
but in real life we're just in folding chairs, sitting
on the Kingdom Hall stage. The first time
I have to give my talk I ask if I can write it myself
without anyone helping.
There are horses and cows in my story even though
the main point is supposed to be
the story of the resurrection.
Say for instance, I write,
we have a cow and a horse that we love.
Is death the end of life for those animals?
When my mother reads those lines,
she shakes her head. *You're getting away from the topic,*
she says. *You have to take the animals out of it, get right*
to the point. Start with people.

I don't know what I am supposed to do
with the fabulous, more interesting part of my story,
where the horses and cows start speaking to me
and to each other. How even though they are old
and won't live much longer, they aren't afraid.
You only have six minutes, my mother says,
and no, you can't get up and walk across the stage
to make your point. Your talk has to be given
sitting down.

So I start again. Rewriting:
Good afternoon, Sister. I'm here to bring you some
good news today.
Did you know God's word is absolute? If we turn to John,
chapter five, verses twenty-eight and twenty-nine . . .

promising myself there'll come a time
when I can use the rest of my story
and stand when I tell it
and give myself and my horses and my cows
a whole lot more time
than six minutes!

first book

There are seven of them,
haikus mostly but rhyming ones, too.
Not enough for a real book until
I cut each page into a small square
staple the squares together, write
one poem
on each page.
Butterflies by Jacqueline Woodson
on the front.

The butterfly book
complete now.

john's bargain store

Down Knickerbocker Avenue is where everyone
on the block goes to shop.
There's a pizzeria if you get hungry,
seventy-five cents a slice.
There's an ice cream shop where cones cost a quarter.
There's a Fabco Shoes store and a beauty parlor.
A Woolworth's five-and-dime and a John's Bargain Store.
For a long time, I don't put one foot inside Woolworth's.
They wouldn't let Black people eat at their lunch counters
in Greenville, I tell Maria.
No way are they getting my money!
So instead, Maria and I go to John's Bargain Store where
three T-shirts cost a dollar. We buy them
in pale pink, yellow and baby blue. Each night
we make a plan:
Wear your yellow one tomorrow, Maria says,
and I'll wear mine.
All year long, we dress alike,
walking up and down Madison Street
waiting for someone to say, *Are you guys cousins?*
so we can smile, say,
Can't you tell from looking at us?!

new girl

Then one day a new girl moves in next door, tells us
her name is Diana and becomes
me and Maria's Second Best Friend in the Whole World.
And even though Maria's mother
knew Diana's mother in Puerto Rico,
Maria promises that doesn't make Diana *más mejor
amiga*—a better friend. But some days, when
it's raining and Mama won't let me go outside,
I see them
on the block, their fingers laced together,
heading around the corner
to the bodega for candy. Those days,
the world feels as gray and cold as it really is
and it's hard
not to believe the new girl isn't *más mejor* than me.
Hard not to believe
my days as Maria's best friend forever and ever amen
are counted.

pasteles & pernil

When Maria's brother, Carlos, gets baptized
he is just a tiny baby in a white lace gown with
so many twenty-dollar bills folded into fans pinned
all over it
that he looks like a green-and-white angel.

Maria and I stand over his crib
talking about all the candy we could buy with just one
of those fans. But we know that God is watching
and don't even dare touch the money.

In the kitchen, there is *pernil* roasting in the oven
the delicious smell filling the house and Maria says,
You should just eat a little bit. But I am not allowed
to eat pork. Instead, I wait for *pasteles* to get
passed around,
wait for the ones her mother has filled with chicken
for Jackie, mi ahijada, wait for the moment when
I can peel the paper
away from the crushed-plantain-covered meat,
break off small pieces with my hands and let the
pastele melt in my mouth. *My mother makes the best*

pasteles in Brooklyn, Maria says. And even though I've
only eaten her mom's, I agree.

Whenever there is the smell of *pernil* and *pasteles* on
the block, we know
there is a celebration going on. And tonight, the party
is at Maria's house. The music is loud and the cake
is big and the *pasteles*
that her mother's been making for three days are

absolutely perfect.

We take our food out to her stoop just as the grown-ups
start dancing merengue, the women lifting their long dresses
to show off their fast-moving feet,
the men clapping and yelling,
Baila! Baila! until the living room floor disappears.
When I ask Maria where Diana is she says,
They're coming later. This part is just for my family.

She pulls the crisp skin
away from the *pernil,* eats the pork shoulder
with rice and beans,
our plates balanced on our laps, tall glasses of Malta
beside us.
and for a long time, neither one of us says anything.

Yeah, I say. *This is only for us. The family.*

curses

We are good kids,
people tell my mother this all the time, say,
You have the most polite children.
I've never heard a bad word from them.

And it's true—we say *please* and *thank you.*
We speak softly. We look adults in the eyes
ask, *How are you?* Bow our heads when we pray.
We don't know how to curse,
when we try to put bad words together they sound strange
like new babies trying to talk and mixing up their sounds.

At home, we aren't allowed words like
stupid or *dumb* or *jerk* or *darn.*
We aren't allowed to say
I hate or *I could die* or *You make me sick.*

We're not allowed to roll our eyes or
look away when my mother is speaking to us.

Once my brother said *butt* and wasn't allowed
to play outside after school for a week.

When we are with our friends and angry, we whisper,
You stupid dummy
and our friends laugh then spew curses
at us like bullets, bend their lips over the words
like they were born speaking them. They coach us on,
tell us to *Just say it!*

But we can't. Even when we try
the words get caught inside our throats, as though
our mother
is standing there waiting, daring them to reach the air.

afros

When Robert comes over with his hair blown out into
an afro, I beg my mother
for the same hairstyle.
Everyone in the neighborhood
has one and all of the black people on *Soul Train*. Even
Michael Jackson and his brothers are all allowed to wear
their hair this way.
Even though she says no to me,
my mom spends a lot of Saturday morning
in her bedroom mirror,
picking her own hair
into a huge black and beautiful dome.
Which
is so completely one hundred percent unfair
but she says, *This is the difference between*
being a grown-up and being a child. When
she's not looking, I stick my tongue out
at her.
My sister catches me, says,
And that's the difference
between being a child and being a grown-up,
like she's twenty years old.
Then rolls her eyes at me and goes back to reading.

graffiti

Your tag is your name written with spray paint
however you want it wherever you want it to be.
It doesn't even have to be
your real name—like Loco who lives on Woodbine Street.
His real name is Orlando but everyone
calls him by his tag so
it's everywhere in Bushwick. Black and red letters and
crazy eyes inside the Os.
Some kids climb to the tops of buildings, hang
over the edge
spray their names upside down from there.

But me and Maria only know the ground, only know
the factory on the corner with its newly painted
bright pink wall. Only know the way my heart jumps
as I press the button down, hear the hiss of paint, watch
J-A-C- begin.

Only know the sound of my uncle's voice,

stopping me before my name is
a part of the history—like the ones on the roofs

and fire escapes and subway cars. I wish
I could explain.
Wish I had the words
to stop his anger, stop the force of him grabbing my hand,
wish I knew how to say,
Just let me write—everywhere!

But my uncle keeps asking over and over again,

What's wrong with you?
Have you lost your mind?
Don't you know people get arrested
for this?

They're just words, I whisper.
They're not trying to hurt anybody!

music

Each morning the radio comes on at seven o'clock.
Sometimes Michael Jackson is singing that A-B-C
is as easy as 1-2-3
or Sly and the Family Stone are thanking us for
letting them
be themselves.
Sometimes it's slower music, the Five Stairsteps
telling us
things are going to get easier, or the Hollies singing,
He ain't heavy, he's my brother
So on we go . . .

My mother lets us choose what music we want
to listen to
as long as the word *funk* doesn't appear anywhere
in the song.
But the summer I am ten, *funk* is in every single song
that comes on the cool black radio stations. So our
mother makes us listen
to the white ones.

All afternoon corny people sing about Colorado,
about everything being beautiful

about how we've only just begun.
My sister falls in love
with the singers but I sneak off
to Maria's house where
safe inside her room with the pink shag carpet
and bunk beds,
we can comb our dolls' hair and sing along when
the Ohio Players say,
He's the funkiest
Worm in the world.
We can dance
the Funky Chicken, tell imaginary intruders
to get the funk out
of our faces. Say the word so hard and so loud
and so many times,
it becomes something different to us—something
    so silly
we laugh just thinking about it.
Funky, funky, funky,
we sing again and again until the word is just a sound
not connected to anything
good or bad
right or wrong.

rikers island

When the phone call comes in the middle of the night,
    it isn't
to tell us someone has died. It's Robert
calling from a prison called Rikers Island.
Even from my half-asleep place,
I can hear my mother taking a heavy breath, whispering,
I knew this was coming, Robert. I knew you weren't
doing right.

In the morning, we eat our cereal in silence as
    our mother tells us
that our uncle won't be around for a while.
When we ask where he's gone, she says, *Jail.*
When we ask why, she says,
It doesn't matter. We love him.
That's all we need to know and keep remembering.
Robert walked the wide road, she says. *And now*
he's paying for it.

Witnesses believe there's a wide road and a narrow road.
To be good in the eyes of God is to walk the narrow one,
live a good clean life, pray, do what's right.

On the wide road, there is every kind of bad thing anyone
can imagine. I imagine my uncle doing his smooth
dance steps down the wide road,
smiling as the music plays loud. I imagine
him laughing, pressing quarters into our palms,
pulling presents for us from his bag, thick gold
bracelet flashing at his wrist.
Where'd you get this? my mother asked, her face tight.
It doesn't matter, my uncle answered. *Y'all know I love you.*

You doing the right thing, Robert? my mother wanted
to know. *Yes,* my uncle said. *I promise you.*

It rains all day. We sit around the house
waiting for the sun to come out so we can go outside.
Dell reads in the corner of our room. I pull out
my beat-up composition notebook
try to write another butterfly poem.
Nothing comes.

The page looks like the day—wrinkled and empty
no longer promising anyone
anything.

moving upstate

From Rikers Island, my uncle is sent
to a prison upstate we can visit.

We don't know what he'll look like, how
much he'll have changed. And because our mother
warns us not to, I don't tell anyone he's in jail.

When my friends ask, I say, *He moved upstate.*
We're going to visit him soon.

He lives in a big house, I say. *With a big yard and everything.*

But the missing settles inside of me. Every time
James Brown comes on the radio, I see Robert dancing.

Every time the commercial for the Crissy doll comes on
I think how I almost got one.

He's my favorite uncle, I say one afternoon.

He's our ONLY uncle, my sister says.
Then goes back to reading.

on the bus
to dannemora

We board the bus when the sun is just kissing the sky.
Darkness like a cape that we wear for hours, curled into it
and back to sleep. From somewhere above us
the O'Jays are singing, telling people all over the world
to join hands and start a love train.
The song rocks me gently into and out of dreaming
and in the dream, a train filled with love goes on and on.

And in the story that begins from the song, the bus
is no longer a bus and we're no longer going to
Dannemora. But there is food and laughter and
the music. The girl telling the story is me but
not me at the same time—watching all of this,
writing it down as fast as she can,
singing along with the O'Jays, asking everyone
to let this train keep on riding . . .
"riding on through . . ."

and it's the story of a whole train filled
with love and how the people on it
aren't in prison but are free to dance
and sing and hug their families whenever they want.

On the bus, some of the people are sleeping, others
are staring out the window or talking softly.
Even the children are quiet. Maybe each of them
    is thinking
their own dream—of daddies and uncles, brothers
    and cousins
one day being free to come on board.

Please don't miss this train at the station
'Cause if you miss it, I feel sorry, sorry for you.

too good

The bus moves slow out of the city until we can see
the mountains, and above that, so much blue sky.

Passing the mountains.

Passing the sea
Passing the heavens.
That's soon where I will be . . .

A song comes to me quickly, the words moving through
my brain and out of my mouth in a whisper but still
my sister hears, asks who taught it to me.

I just made it up, I say.

No you didn't, she says back. *It's too good. Someone
taught that to you.*

I don't say anything back. Just look out the window
and smile.

Too good, I am thinking. The stuff I make up is *too good.*

dannemora

At the gate of the prison, guards glare at us, then slowly
allow us in.

My big brother is afraid.
He looks up at the barbed wire
puts his hands in his pockets.
I know he wishes he was home with his chemistry set.
I know he wants to be anywhere but here.
Nothing but stone and a big building that goes so far up
and so far back and forth that we can't see
where the beginning is
or where it might end. Gray brick, small windows
covered with wire. Who could see
out from here? The guards check our pockets,
check our bags, make us
walk through X-ray machines.

My big brother holds out his arms. Lets the guards pat him
from shoulder to ankle, checking
for anything he might be hiding . . .
He is Hope Austin Woodson the Second, part of a long line
of Woodsons—doctors and lawyers and teachers—

but as quickly as THAT! he can become
a number. Like Robert Leon Irby is now
so many numbers across the pocket
of his prison uniform that it's hard
not to keep looking at them,
waiting for them to morph into letters
that spell out
my uncle's name.

not robert

When the guard brings our uncle to the waiting room
that is filled with other families
waiting, he is not
Robert. His afro is gone now,
shaved to a black shadow on his perfect skull.
His eyebrows are thicker than I remember, dipping down
in a newer, sadder way. Even when he smiles,
opens his arms
to hug all of us at once, the bit I catch of it, before
jumping into his hug, is a half smile, caught
and trapped inside a newer, sadder
uncle.

mountain song

On the way home from visiting Robert,
I watch the mountains move past me
and slowly the mountain song starts coming again
more words this time, coming faster
than I can sing them.

Passing the mountains
Passing the sea
Passing the heavens
waiting for me.

Look at the mountains
Such a beautiful sea
And there's a promise that heaven
is filled with glory.

I sing the song over and over again,
quietly into the windowpane, my forehead
pressed against the cool glass. Tears coming fast now.
The song makes me think of Robert and Daddy
   and Greenville

and everything that feels far behind me now, everything
that is going

or already gone.

I am thinking if I can hold on to the memory of this song
get home and write it down, then it will happen,
I'll be a writer. I'll be able to hold on to
each moment, each memory
everything.

poem on paper

When anyone in the family asks
what I'm writing, I usually say,
Nothing
or
A story
or
A poem
and only my mother says,
Just so long as you're not writing about our family.

And I'm not.

Well, not really . . .

Up in the mountains
far from the sea
there's a place called Dannemora
the men are not free . . .

daddy

It is early spring
when my grandmother sends for us.

Warm enough to believe again
that food will come from the newly thawed earth.
This is the weather, my mother says, *Daddy loved
to garden in.* We arrive
not long before my grandfather is about to take
his last breaths,
breathless ourselves from our first ride
in an airplane.

I want to tell him all about it
how loud it was when the plane lifted into the sky,
each of us, leaning toward the window,
watching New York
grow small and speckled beneath us.
How the meals arrived
on tiny trays—some kind of fish that none of us ate.
I want to tell him how the stewardess gave us wings
to pin to our blouses and shirts and told Mama
we were beautiful and well behaved. But

my grandfather is sleeping when we come to his bedside,
opens his eyes only to smile, turns so that my grandmother
can press ice cubes against his lips. She tells us,
He needs his rest now. That evening
he dies.

On the day he is buried, my sister and I wear white dresses,
the boys in white shirts and ties.
We walk slowly through Nicholtown, a long parade
    of people
who loved him—Hope, Dell, Roman and me
leading it. This is how we bury our dead—a silent parade
through the streets, showing the world our sadness, others
who knew my grandfather joining in on the walk,
children waving,
grown-ups dabbing at their eyes.

Ashes to ashes, we say at the grave site
with each handful of dirt we drop gently onto
    his lowering casket.
We will see you in the by and by, we say.
We will see you in the by and by.

how to listen #7

Even the silence
has a story to tell you.
Just listen. Listen.

PART V

ready
to change
the
world

after greenville #2

After Daddy dies
my grandmother sells the house in Nicholtown
gives the brown chair to Miss Bell,
Daddy's clothes to the Brothers at the Kingdom Hall,
the kitchen table and bright yellow chairs
to her sister Lucinda in Fieldcrest Village.

After Daddy dies
my grandmother brings the bed our mother was born in
to Brooklyn. Unpacks her dresses
in the small empty bedroom
downstairs,
puts her Bible, *Watchtowers* and *Awakes*,
a picture of Daddy
on the little brown bookshelf.

After Daddy dies
spring blurs into summer
then winter comes on too cold and fast,
and my grandmother moves a chair to the living room
window
watches the tree drop the last of its leaves

while boys play skelly and spinning tops in the middle
of our quiet Brooklyn street.

After Daddy dies
I learn to jump double Dutch slowly
tripping again and again over my too-big feet. Counting,
Ten, twenty, thirty, forty deep into the winter until
one afternoon
gravity releases me and my feet fly free in the ropes,
fifty, sixty, seventy, eighty, ninety . . .

as my grandmother watches me.
Both of our worlds
changed forever.

mimosa tree

A mimosa tree, green and thin limbed, pushes up through
the snow. My grandmother brought the seeds with her
   from *back home.*

Sometimes, she pulls a chair to the window, looks
   down over the yard.

The promise of glittering sidewalks feels a long time
   behind us now, no diamonds anywhere to be found.

But some days, just after snow falls,
the sun comes out, shines down on the promise
of that tree from *back home* joining us here.

Shines down over the bright white ground.

And on those days, so much light and warmth fills
the room that it's hard not to believe
in a little bit

of everything.

bubble-gum cigarettes

You can buy a box of bubble-gum cigarettes for a dime
at the bodega around the corner.
Sometimes, Maria and I walk there,
our fingers laced together, a nickel
in each of our pockets.

The bubble gum is pink with white paper
wrapped around it. When you put it in your mouth
and blow, a white puff comes out.
You can really believe
you're smoking.

We talk with the bubble-gum cigarettes
between our fingers. Hold them in the air
like the movie stars on TV. We let them dangle
from our mouths and look at each other
through slitted eyes
then laugh at how grown-up we can be
how beautiful.

When my sister sees us
pretending to smoke, she shakes her head.
That's why Daddy died, she says.

After that
me and Maria peel the paper off,
turn our cigarettes into regular bubble gum.
After that
the game is over.

what's left behind

You've got your daddy's easy way,
my grandmother says to me, holding
the picture of my grandfather
in her hands. *I watch you with*
your friends and see him all over again.

Where will the wedding supper be?
Way down yonder in a hollow tree . . .

We look at the picture without talking.
Sometimes, I don't know the words for things,
how to write down the feeling of knowing
that every dying person leaves something behind.

I got my grandfather's easy way. Maybe
I know this when I'm laughing. Maybe
I know it when I think of Daddy
and he feels close enough
for me to lay my head against his shoulder.

I remember how he laughed, I tell my grandmother
and she smiles and says,

Because you laugh just like him.
Two peas in a pod, you were.

Two peas in a pod we were.

the stories i tell

Every autumn, the teacher asks us to
write about summer vacation
and read it to the class.

In Brooklyn, everybody goes south
or to Puerto Rico
or to their cousin's house in Queens.

But after my grandmother moves to New York,
we only go down south once,
for my aunt Lucinda's funeral. After that,
my grandmother says she's done with the South
says it makes her too sad.

But now
when summer comes

our family gets on a plane, flies
to

Africa
Hawaii
Chicago.

For summer vacation we went to Long Island,
to the beach. Everybody went fishing and everybody
caught a lot of fish.

Even though no one in my family has ever been
to Long Island
or fished
or likes the ocean—too deep, too scary. Still,
each autumn, I write a story.

In my writing, there is a stepfather now
who lives in California but meets us wherever we go.
There is a church, not a Kingdom Hall.
There is a blue car, a new dress, loose unribboned hair.

In my stories, our family is regular as air
two boys, two girls, sometimes a dog.

Did that really happen? the kids in class ask.

Yeah, I say. *If it didn't, how would I know what to write?*

how to listen #8

Do you remember . . . ?
someone's always asking and
someone always does.

fate & faith & reasons

Everything happens for a reason, my mother
says. Then tells me how Kay believed
in fate and destiny—everything
that ever happened or was going to happen
couldn't ever be avoided. The marchers
down south didn't just up and start
their marching—it was part of a longer, bigger
plan, that maybe belonged to God.

My mother tells me this as we fold laundry, white towels
separated from the colored ones. Each
a threat to the other and I remember the time
I spilled bleach on a blue towel, dotting it forever.
The pale pink towel, a memory
of when it was washed with a red one. Maybe
there is something, after all, to the way
some people want to remain—each to its own kind.
But in time
maybe
everything will fade to gray.

Even all of us coming to Brooklyn,

my mother says, *wasn't some accident.* And I can't help
thinking of the birds here—how they disappear
in the wintertime,
heading south for food and warmth and shelter.
Heading south
to stay alive . . . passing us on the way . . .

No accidents, my mother says. *Just fate and faith*
and reasons.

When I ask my mother what she believes in,
she stops, midfold, and looks out the back window.

    Autumn

is full on here and the sky is bright blue.

I guess I believe in right now, she says. *And the resurrection.*
And Brooklyn. And the four of you.

what if . . . ?

Maria's mother never left Bayamón, Puerto Rico,
and my mother never left Greenville.

What if no one had ever walked the grassy fields
that are now Madison Street and said,
Let's put some houses here.

What if the people in Maria's building didn't sell
1279 Madison Street
to Maria's parents
and our landlord told my mom that he couldn't rent
1283
to someone who already had four children.

What if the park with the swings wasn't right across
Knickerbocker Avenue?

What if Maria hadn't walked out of her building
one day and said,
My name is Maria but my mom calls me Googoo.
What if I had laughed instead of saying,

You're lucky. I wish I had a nickname, too.
You want to go to the park sometime?

What if she didn't have a sister and two brothers
and I didn't have a sister and two brothers
and her dad didn't teach us to box
and her mother didn't cook such good food?

I can't even imagine any of it, Maria says.

Nope, I say. *Neither can I.*

bushwick history lesson

Before German mothers wrapped scarves around
 their heads,
kissed their own mothers good-bye and headed across
 the world
to Bushwick—

Before the Italian fathers sailed across the ocean
for the dream of America
and found themselves in Bushwick—

Before Dominican daughters donned quinceañera
 dresses and walked proudly down Bushwick Avenue—

Before young brown boys in cutoff shorts spun their
 first tops and played their first games of skelly on
 Bushwick Streets—

Before any of that, this place was called *Boswijck,*

settled by the Dutch
and Franciscus the Negro, a former slave
who bought his freedom.

And all of New York was called New Amsterdam,
    run by a man
named Peter Stuyvesant. There were slaves here.
Those who could afford to own
their freedom
lived on the other side of the wall.
And now that place is called Wall Street.

When my teacher says, *So write down what all of this means
to you,* our heads bend over our notebooks, the whole class
silent. The whole class belonging somewhere:
Bushwick.

I didn't just appear one day.
I didn't just wake up and know how to write my name.

I keep writing, knowing now
that I was a long time coming.

how to listen #9

Under the back porch
there's an alone place I go
writing all I've heard.

the promise land

When my uncle gets out of jail
he isn't just my uncle anymore, he is
Robert the Muslim and wears
a small black *kufi* on his head.

And even though we know
we Witnesses are the chosen ones, we listen
to the stories he tells about
a man named Muhammad
and a holy place called Mecca
and the strength of all Black people.

We sit in a circle around him, his hands
moving slow through the air, his voice
calmer and quieter than it was before
he went away.

When he pulls out a small rug to pray on
I kneel beside him, wanting to see
his Mecca
wanting to know the place
he calls the Promise Land.

Look with your heart and your head, he tells me
his own head bowed.
It's out there in front of you.
You'll know when you get there.

power to the people

On the TV screen a woman
named Angela Davis is telling us
there's a revolution going on and that it's time

for Black people to defend themselves.

So Maria and I walk through the streets,
our fists raised in the air Angela Davis style.

We read about her in the *Daily News,* run
to the television each time she's interviewed.

She is beautiful and powerful and has
my same gap-toothed smile. We dream
of running away to California
to join the Black Panthers
the organization Angela is a part of.

She is not afraid, she says,
to die for what she believes in
but doesn't plan to die
without a fight.

The FBI says Angela Davis is one of America's
Most Wanted.

Already, there are so many things I don't understand, why
someone would have to die
or even fight for what they believe in.

Why the cops would want someone who is trying
to change the world
in jail.

We are not afraid to die, Maria and I shout, fists high,
for what we believe in.
But both of us know—we'd rather keep believing
and live.

say it loud

My mother tells us the Black Panthers are doing
all kinds of stuff
to make the world a better place for Black children.

In Oakland, they started a free breakfast program
so that poor kids can have a meal
before starting their school day. Pancakes,
toast, eggs, fruit: we watch the kids eat happily,
sing songs about how proud they are
to be Black. We sing the song along with them
stand on the bases of lampposts and scream,
Say it loud: I'm Black and I'm proud until
my mother hollers from the window,
Get down before you break your neck.

I don't understand the revolution.
In Bushwick, there's a street we can't cross called
Wyckoff Avenue. White people live on the other side.
Once a boy from my block got beat up for walking
over there.
Once there were four white families on our block
but they all moved away except for the old lady

who lives by the tree. Some days, she brings out cookies
tells us stories of the old neighborhood when everyone
was German or Irish and even some Italians
down by Wilson Avenue.
All kinds of people, she says. And the cookies
are too good for me to say,

Except us.

Everyone knows where they belong here.
It's not Greenville

but it's not diamond sidewalks either.

I still don't know what it is
that would make people want to get along.

Maybe no one does.

Angela Davis smiles, gap-toothed and beautiful,
    raises her fist in the air
says, *Power to the people,* looks out from the television

directly into my eyes.

maybe mecca

There is a teenager on our block with one arm missing,
we call him Leftie and he tells us
he lost his arm in Vietnam.
That's a war, he says. *Y'all lucky to be too young to go.*
It doesn't hurt anymore, he tells us when we gather
around him.
But his eyes are sad eyes and some days he walks
around the block
maybe a hundred times without saying anything
to anyone.
When we call, *Hey Leftie!* he doesn't even look our way.

Some evenings, I kneel toward Mecca with my uncle.
Maybe Mecca
is the place Leftie goes to in his mind, when
the memory of losing
his arm becomes too much. Maybe Mecca is
good memories,
presents and stories and poetry and *arroz con pollo*
and family and friends . . .

Maybe Mecca is the place everyone is looking for . . .

It's out there in front of you, my uncle says.

I know I'll know it
when I get there.

the revolution

Don't wait for your school to teach you, my uncle says,
about the revolution. It's happening in the streets.

He's been out of jail for more than a year now and his hair
is an afro again, gently moving in the wind as we head
to the park, him holding tight
to my hand even when we're not crossing
Knickerbocker Avenue, even now when I'm too old
for hand holding *and the like.*

The revolution is when Shirley Chisholm ran for president
and the rest of the world tried to imagine
a Black woman in the White House.

When I hear the word
revolution
I think of the carousel with
all those beautiful horses
going around as though they'll never stop and me
choosing the purple one each time, climbing up onto it
and reaching for the golden ring, as soft music plays.

The revolution is always going to be happening.

I want to write this down, that the revolution is like
a merry-go-round, history always being made
somewhere. And maybe for a short time,
we're a part of that history. And then the ride stops
and our turn is over.

We walk slow toward the park where I can already see
the big swings, empty and waiting for me.

And after I write it down, maybe I'll end it this way:

My name is Jacqueline Woodson
and I am ready for the ride.

how to listen #10

Write down what I think
I know. The knowing will come.

Just keep listening . . .

a writer

You're a writer, Ms. Vivo says,
her gray eyes bright behind
thin wire frames. Her smile bigger than anything
so I smile back, happy to hear these words
from a teacher's mouth. She is a feminist, she tells us
and thirty fifth-grade hands bend into desks
where our dictionaries wait to open yet another
world to us. Ms. Vivo pauses, watches our fingers fly
Webster's has our answers.
Equal rights, a boy named Andrew yells out.
For women.
My hands freeze on the thin white pages.
Like Blacks, Ms. Vivo, too, is part of a revolution.

But right now, that revolution is so far away from me.
This moment, this *here,* this *right now* is my teacher
  saying,
You're a writer, as she holds the poem I am just beginning.
The first four lines, stolen
from my sister:

Black brothers, Black sisters, all of them were great
no fear no fright but a willingness to fight . . .

You can have them, Dell said when she saw.
I don't want to be a poet.

And then my own pencil moving late into the evening:

In big fine houses lived the whites
in little old shacks lived the blacks
but the blacks were smart
in fear they took no part.
One of them was Martin
with a heart of gold.

You're a writer, Ms. Vivo says, holding my poem out to me.

And standing in front of the class
taking my poem from her
my voice shakes as I recite the first line:

Black brothers, Black sisters, all of them were great. . . .

But my voice grows stronger with each word because
more than anything else in the world,
I want to believe her.

every wish, one dream

Every dandelion blown
each *Star light, star bright,*
The first star I see tonight.

My wish is always the same.

Every fallen eyelash
and first firefly of summer . . .

The dream remains.

What did you wish for?
To be a writer.

Every heads-up penny found
and daydream and night dream
and even when people say it's a pipe dream . . . !

I want to be a writer.

Every sunrise and sunset and song
against a cold windowpane.

Passing the mountains.

Passing the sea.

Every story read
every poem remembered:

I loved my friend
and
When I see birches bend to left and right
and
"Nay," answered the child: "but these are the wounds of Love."

Every memory . . .

Froggie went a-courting, and he did ride
Uh hmm.

brings me closer
and closer to the dream.

the earth from far away

Every Saturday morning, we run downstairs
to the television. Just as the theme song
from *The Big Blue Marble* begins, the four of us sing along:

The earth's a big blue marble when you see it from out there.

Then the camera is zooming in on that marble,
    the blue becoming
water, then land, then children in Africa and Texas
    and China
and Spain and sometimes, New York City! The world
close enough to touch now and children from all over
right in our living room! Telling us their stories.

The sun and moon declare, our beauty's very rare . . .

The world—*my* world!—like words. Once
there was only the letter *J* and my sister's hand
wrapped around mine, guiding me, promising me
infinity. This big blue marble
of world and words and people and places

inside my head and

somewhere out there, too.

All of it, mine now if I just listen

and write it down.

what i believe

I believe in God and evolution.
I believe in the Bible and the Qur'an.
I believe in Christmas and the New World.
I believe that there is good in each of us
no matter who we are or what we believe in.
I believe in the words of my grandfather.
I believe in the city and the South
the past and the present.
I believe in Black people and White people coming
    together.
I believe in nonviolence and "Power to the People."
I believe in my little brother's pale skin and my own
    dark brown.
I believe in my sister's brilliance and the too-easy
    books I love to read.
I believe in my mother on a bus and Black people
    refusing to ride.
I believe in good friends and good food.

I believe in johnny pumps and jump ropes,
Malcolm and Martin, Buckeyes and Birmingham,

writing and listening, bad words and good words—
I believe in Brooklyn!

I believe in one day and someday and this
    perfect moment called *Now*.

each world

When there are many worlds
you can choose the one
you walk into each day.

You can imagine yourself brilliant as your sister,
slower moving, quiet and thoughtful as your older brother
or filled up with the hiccupping joy and laughter
of the baby in the family.

You can imagine yourself a mother now, climbing
onto a bus at nightfall, turning
to wave good-bye to your children, watching
the world of South Carolina disappear behind you.

When there are many worlds, love can wrap itself
around you, say, *Don't cry.* Say, *You are as good as anyone.*
Say, *Keep remembering me.* And you know, even as the
    world explodes
around you—that you are loved . . .

Each day a new world
opens itself up to you. And all the worlds you are—

Ohio and Greenville
Woodson and Irby
Gunnar's child and Jack's daughter
Jehovah's Witness and nonbeliever
listener and writer
Jackie and Jacqueline—

gather into one world

called You

where You decide

what each world
and each story
and each ending

will finally be.

author's note

Memory is strange. When I first began to write *Brown Girl Dreaming*, my childhood memories of Greenville came flooding back to me—small moments and bigger ones, too. Things I hadn't thought about in years and other stuff I've never forgotten. When I began to write it all down, I realized how much I missed the South. So for the first time in many years, I returned "home," and saw cousins I hadn't seen since I was small, heard stories I had heard many times from my grandmother, walked roads that were very different now but still the same roads of my childhood. It was a bittersweet journey. I wish I could have walked those roads again with my mom, my grandfather, my uncle Robert, my aunt Kay, and my grandmother. But all have made their own journey to the next place. So I walked the roads alone this time. Still, it felt as though each of them was with me—they're all deeply etched now, into memory.

And that's what this book is—my past, my people, my memories, my story.

I knew I couldn't write about the South without writing about Ohio. And even though I was only a baby when we lived there, I have the gift of my amazing aunt Ada

Adams, who is a genealogist and our family historian. She was my go-to person and filled in so many gaps in my memory. Aunt Ada took me right back to Columbus. During the writing of this book, I returned to Ohio with my family. Aunt Ada took us on a journey of the Underground Railroad, showed us the graves of grandparents and great-grandparents, told me so much history I had missed out on as a child. Aunt Ada not only showed me the past but she also helped me understand the present. So often, I am asked where my stories come from. I know now my stories are part of a continuum—my aunt is a storyteller. So were my mom and my grandmother. And the history Aunt Ada showed me—the rich history that is *my* history—made me at once proud and thoughtful. The people who came before me worked so hard to make this world a better place for me. I know my work is to make the world a better place for those coming after. As long as I can remember this, I can continue to do the work I was put here to do.

On the journey to writing this book, my dad, Jack Woodson, chimed in when he could. Even as I write this, I smile because my father always makes me laugh. I like to think I acquired a bit of his sense of humor. I didn't know him for many years. When I met him again at the age of fourteen, it was as though a puzzle piece had dropped from the air and landed right where it belonged. My dad is that puzzle piece.

Gaps were also filled in by my friend Maria, who

helped the journey along with pictures and stories. When we were little, we used to say we'd one day be old ladies together, sitting in rocking chairs remembering our childhood and laughing. We've been friends for nearly five decades now and still call each other My Forever Friend. I hope everyone has a Forever Friend in their life.

But at the end of the day, I was alone with *Brown Girl Dreaming*—walking through these memories and making sense out of myself as a writer in a way I had never done before.

I am often asked if I had a hard life growing up. I think my life was very complicated and very rich. Looking back on it, I think my life was at once ordinary and amazing. I couldn't imagine any other life. I know that I was lucky enough to be born during a time when the world was changing like crazy—and that I was a part of that change. I know that I was and continue to be loved.

I couldn't ask for anything more.

thankfuls

I am thankful for my memory. When it needed help on the journey, I am also thankful for my fabulous editor, Nancy Paulsen. More help came from Sara LaFleur. This book wouldn't be in the world without my family, including Hope, Odella, and Roman, Toshi, Jackson-Leroi, and Juliet—thank you for your patience and thorough reading and rereading. Thanks to my forever friend, Maria Cortez-Ocasio, her husband, Sam, and her daughters Jillian, Samantha, and Angelina. Even her grandson, Little Sammy. And of course, her mom, Darma—thanks for feeding me so well over the years.

Toshi Reagon, thanks for reading this and sitting with me as I fretted over it. Thanks for your music, your guidance, your stories.

On the Ohio side: a big big thank-you to my aunt Ada— genealogist extraordinaire!—and to my aunt Alicia and my uncle David and, of course, my dad, Jack Woodson.

On the Greenville side: big thanks to my cousins Michael and Sheryl Irby, Megan Irby, Michael and Kenneth Sullivan, Dorothy Vaughn-Welch, Samuel Miller, La'Brandon, Monica Vaughn, and all my other relatives who opened their doors, let me in, told me their stories!

In North Carolina, thanks so much to Stephanie Grant, Ara Wilson, Augusta, and Josephine for that fabulously quiet guest room and dinner at the end of the day for many days until this book was close to being in the world.

On the Brooklyn and Vermont sides: thanks to my village. So grateful for all of you!

In memory: thanks to my mom, Mary Anne Woodson, my uncles Odell and Robert Irby, my grandmother Georgiana Scott Irby, my grandfather Gunnar Irby, and my aunt Hallique Caroline (Kay) Irby.

These thankfuls wouldn't be complete without acknowledging the myriad teachers who, in many different ways, pointed this brown girl toward her dream.

jacqueline
as a child

jacqueline's parents

Mama pretty

Jack

Mama

Mama and Jack's wedding

332

Hope

Odella

Roman

jacqueline's
siblings

the woodsons
of ohio

Grandpa
Hope

grandma Grace

Jack

Uncle David

Aunt Ann

Aunt Alicia

Aunt Ada

grandpa
gunnar
(Daddy)

the irbys
of south carolina

Aunt Caroline (Kay)

Grandma Georgiana

Mama

Uncle Odell

Uncle Robert